Camel-Makers

Building Effective
Teacher Teams Together

A Modern Fable for Educators

Camel-Makers

Building Effective Teacher Teams Together

by

Daniel L. Kain

National Middle School Association

Westerville, Ohio

National Middle School Association
4151 Executive Parkway, Suite 300
Westerville, Ohio 43081
Telephone (800) 528-NMSA
www.nmsa.org

Second Printing, May 2002

COVER AND ILLUSTRATIONS BY BARBARA BRANNON
PRINTED IN THE UNITED STATES OF AMERICA

Sue Swaim, Executive Director
Jeff Ward, Director of Business Services
John Lounsbury, Senior Editor, Professional Publications
Edward Brazee, Associate Editor, Professional Publications
Mary Mitchell, Copy Editor/Designer
Marcia Meade-Hurst, Senior Publications Representative
ISBN: 1-56090-151-9   NMSA Stock Number: 1248

Library of Congress Cataloging-in-Publication Data

Kain, Daniel L., date
    Camel makers: building effective teacher teams together: a
modern fable for educators/by Daniel L. Kain.
        p. cm.
    Includes bibliographical references (p.).
    ISBN 1-56090-151-9 (pbk.)
    1. Teaching teams--United States.   I. Title
LB1029.T4K35   1998
371.14'8--dc21   98-11993
                                                    CIP

. . . to my family, who supported me through all the research. Thanks to Kerry, Erik, Kelcy, and Taylor. Thanks, too, to Joe Belanger, who guided me through so many studies, to Jan Ophus, who introduced me to the middle school, and to John Lounsbury, who believed in the camel- makers.

About the Author

Daniel L. Kain began his teaching career at a junior high school. As that school moved to the middle school model he experienced the power of working in a dynamic, if challenging, team. He has researched teaming at various levels, with articles on teaming appearing in such publications as *Middle School Journal; Research in Middle Level Education Quarterly; We Gain More Than We Give: Teaming in Middle Schools; Schools In the Middle – The Early Adolescent Magazine; Journal of Curriculum and Supervision;* and *Teachers College Record.* Dr. Kain is currently a member of a teaching team for secondary/middle school teacher preparation at Northern Arizona University in Flagstaff, where he enjoys hiking with his wife and three children.

Contents

A Fable for Our Times

Never before have the real "gut" issues of teaming been presented in such an engaging and enlightening way as they are in this modern fable for middle level educators – a fanciful account of finding and sharing the "Jamal papers," the minutes of that first committee thousands of years ago that created a camel by reconstituting a horse. This tale provides the means of bringing front and center such concerns as team isolation, personality conflicts, and lack of leadership. The wise and learned Dr. Drapolemac, after years of studying the Jamal script, offers analysis and interpretation to focus team issues on middle school concerns, including activities for teams to put these ideas into action.

Daniel Kain has provided a clever, effective way to examine the inner workings of teams. His intimate knowledge of humans and how they function in team settings is evident, while the hypothetical nature of the fable provides a safe context for honestly assessing a team's processes. There is realism and meat here despite the fiction and bits of levity.

This publication is particularly timely, for it is now recognized that teams all too generally reach and rest on a plateau that is far short of the long-term goals for which teams are created. While many benefits of teaming are quickly realized and teachers so organized, with rare exceptions, become highly supportive of teaming, experience in the last two decades makes it apparent that too often teams do not continue their efforts to develop a common vision, integrate the curriculum, and institute new ways to increase student achievement. This unique resource will assist teams in critiquing their status, taking action to improve it, and all the while enjoying the task. The now substantial body of literature on teaming has an addition unlike anything presently available. Enjoy it — and learn from it.

— John H. Lounsbury

"A camel looks like a horse designed by a committee."
— *Vogue* Magazine, 1958

"I should be on such a committee!"
—J.S. Drapolemac

1.

Discovery of a Priceless Document

A New Look at Teams

T he wind shifted. Sergeant Angelina Castillo pulled herself tighter into her windbreaker. She concentrated on pushing down, down into the sand, away from the biting power of the desert wind.

I hate this, she thought. *I'm tired of the heat, tired of the dirt, tired of the war. My feet are sore, and there's something poking into my back.*

But what do you do? Wait. When the sand storm ended, Sergeant Castillo began to dig herself out of her newly formed mound. As she reached her hand back to touch the sore spot on her back, her hand encountered a strange shape – smooth, large, out-of-place from her experience in the desert. She struggled to dig it out, her face pressed into the suffocating sand, but her curiosity driving her on. Castillo emerged from the mound with what would prove to be one of the most important discoveries of the century: the Jamal script. Of course, all she saw was a rather plain, cracked pot. But in the hands of archeolinguists, this cracked pot yielded the records of the design team that produced what has been come to be known as the camel.

The commentary

The tortuous intrigue involved in the acquisition and preservation of this document, the political machinations needed to bring the text to the attention of the academic world, and the difficulties of translation would in themselves make stories worthy of a mini-series. However, this book will recount the less sensational, but more enduring, story revealed by the Jamal script itself. What can we, as people who work in the world of teams and cooperative ventures, learn from this, the earliest recorded human committee? What lessons await us in the Jamal script?

A matter of such importance requires delicate consideration. Therefore, this book has tried to bring before its readers the most useful and least imposing structure possible. Rather than merely presenting the script or someone's view of the document, this book offers the unique format of selected transcriptions from the actual meetings of the Jamal group, with commentary by one of the most renowned authorities in the field of human cooperation, Dr. J.S. Drapolemac. Dr. Drapolemac's insight into the experiences of the Jamal group will, we believe, aid any reader in grasping the full significance of this priceless document. Dr. Drapolemac has spent the last three years in careful study of the Jamal scripts, bringing to the text both linguistic expertise and vast amounts of scholarship in collaborative working arrangements. Through his commentary, the wisdom of the ancient world and modern science combine into a rich portrait of possibilities for today's teams.

As a special bonus, Dr. Drapolemac has agreed to focus his commentary in such a way that members of middle school teams will be the primary beneficiaries of his insights. For about three decades, middle school advocates have argued for the team structure as the best way to serve students in the middle grades (Erb, 1997). Recent literature has highlighted the role of teams in middle schools (Dickinson & Erb, 1997; Irvin, 1997), providing many insights into the practice of teaming. Dr. D adds to our understanding by bringing together the three worlds of business teaming, middle school practices (he has spent time observing middle school teams, reading the literature, and talking to middle school teachers), and the Jamal script. What was already a treasure chest of understanding becomes even richer for us with this middle school focus. While the presentation here includes only portions of the Jamal script, we believe it will provide readers with insight and assistance in teaming.

The Camel-Makers

2.

"What's This Thing Supposed To Do?"

Teaming for a Purpose

Dr. D's Introductory Note

What follows is an amazing document. Rarely in human life do we have the opportunity to glimpse the inner workings of those who create our most treasured artifacts. What debates did the designers of the Sphinx conduct? We don't know. How did the architects of the Taj Mahal come to agreement? We haven't a clue. Who suggested the Aztecan calendar? Unfortunately, that's something we'll never be able to determine. What was the tribe's plan for roofing Stonehenge? Mystery!

But we have in these pages the happy record of the original group that created that most marvelous breed of animals - the camel! Of the group's origin we know precious little. Appointed, it would seem, the members entered their labors enthusiastically. As the text will make clear, however, their work was not without conflict and struggle. We know virtually nothing about their private lives, but the five members of the Jamal group - Melchuzar, Sichem, Dina, Rachel, and Berodak - come to life in the transcripts of their work. And who, we ask, served as clerk to these important deliberations? That, I'm afraid, remains a mystery, too.

You will find what follows to be organized in the simplest way possible. The translations of the original minutes of the camel-makers are listed first in each chapter. These are unchanged, though certain portions have been deleted due to space considerations. In boxes or marginal notes accompanying the original minutes, you will find my brief comments on the work. I try to draw attention to key points, though to a large degree, the minutes speak for themselves.

Following each transcription, I include a brief commentary on that segment of notes. In some cases, I cite works that reflect the experience of the camel-makers. I am fascinated by the Jamal anticipators, those who uncovered similar ideas without the benefit of this amazing discovery. My readers will forgive me if this appears too stuffy and scholarly. However, I find it curious that current researchers and authors reveal ideas that were present in documents that have been hidden for more than two millennia. I cannot help but highlight such curiosities. Also, I occasionally suggest practices or activities for teams wishing to emulate the Jamal Group. My own feeling is that a team can profit best by working with some of the ideas immediately, though I can understand the desire to hurry through the actual record. Without further delay, then, I give you the minutes of the Jamal group!

THE COMMITTEE:

Melchuzar, Chair

Dina

Sichem

Berodak

Rachel

The minutes

Melchuzar: Welcome! This most noble gathering promises to bring light and joy in the lives of our people. This opportunity presents us with challenges never met before. As the saying goes, "The winds of the moment bring ..."

Dina: Cut it, Melchuzar. We've got work to do.

Melchuzar: The tongue of wisdom is indeed short and sharp. Right. Let's begin.

Already you can see that Dina takes on the role of keeping the group focused. Is she a little brisk?

Sichem: Begin what? I'm still not quite sure about what we're doing here.

Berodak: That's a great start for us. The most important job given out, and we're not sure why we're here.

Sichem: I mean, I know we're supposed to make an animal, but ...

Melchuzar: Not make, my friend. We are not in a position to make anything. Our task is to, what's the word?

Dina: Design. We're supposed to design it.

Melchuzar: Of course. We must design the beast of perfection, the glory of the desert, the salvation of the ...

Dina: We get the idea.

Berodak: It's fantastic. We can control everything!

Rachel: New colors, that's what I think. Every animal seems to fall roughly into shades of brown and black and white. Why not think about something, say, in blue? Have you thought of that? We could make the azure skies wander the dunes!

Melchuzar: And sizes. What vistas open here! Endless is the desert! Do we wish this to be a pillar in the desert, a mark for the weary eye to cling to, or do we choose the smallest beauty, a toy for the hands?

Rachel: Wings, I say. Why not skim over the sands, wind rushing past the skin.

Dina: Okay, okay. Let's get at it.

Berodak: Wait a minute. Think about the opportunity here. I say we can completely alter the way commerce is carried out for our people. Why not rethink the basics of our existence? Why not—

Sichem: We'll be famous! It won't be long before we'll be able to go anywhere and have crowds of people gathering to hear from us.

Melchuzar: We could write a scroll! If we are able, as the saying goes, to "make the oasis of joy boundless," we will soon find riches for our memoirs.

Berodak: This is great. We just need more support. Do you think we should spend some time discussing the ways we could get help to do all this?

Rachel: Yes. Let's do. I already envision that we may be able to resolve the conflicts we've begun to see lately among the various bands that have separated throughout the region. Surely there could be no better way to make our mark than to bring some harmony.

Melchuzar: Indeed. It is, as one hears all the time, —

Dina: HOLD IT!

Berodak: Don't get so upset. You're cutting off some productive discussion in an angry tone.

What's happening here is delightful! The Jamal members are beginning to engage in imaginative, fanciful idea generation. It may not be the best time, but it's something we want to look at more closely later.

Dina: I know it. But we're wandering far off here.

Melchuzar: Surely you don't dismiss the importance of harmony and cooperation. Surely you see value in our names carrying on for years after our deaths. You can't tell me the idea of rethinking our people's existence is not important!

Dina: No. I don't dismiss or devalue or disagree. But all that is not our reason to gather together. Were we not given a job?

Sichem: That's what I wanted to know.

Rachel: Of course we were. You know it.

Dina: Then where are we headed with this? Let's get at our job.

Berodak: Maybe you'd care to define what that job is? After all, you're the only one concerned about it.

Dina: I think we all should be concerned about it. We have to draw some limits here, or we'll never know what we've accomplished. So here's the question: what's this thing supposed to do?

Do you see the danger the team is in here? Where's all this going?

Melchuzar: The animal, you mean?

Dina: Yes. What's it supposed to do?

Rachel: I guess it's a kind of horse. So it's supposed to transport people and stuff.

Berodak: Well that doesn't make a whole lot of sense. If we've got a horse, why another one?

Dina: That's my point. It's supposed to do something different, or else we're wasting our time.

Rachel: But weren't we getting at that with colors and other ideas?

Dina: I don't think so. I think what we were getting at was putting off our real task. What's it supposed to do? Not look like, do.

Melchuzar: You speak well, Dina. Our charge was to create the beast to bring prosperity and happiness to our people. Everything we speak of should focus on that. So, it must be a beast that can—

Sichem: Carry great weights.

Rachel: Walk long distances?

Berodak: Provide materials for the people.

Dina: Function with very little water.

Melchuzar: Resist the sand storms.

Rachel: Make beautiful sounds.

Dina: Beautiful sounds?

Rachel: Why not?

Melchuzar: Then we have a guiding idea: our discussions focus on how we can design a beast to meet all the requirements of desert travel. That's our purpose!

Commentary

Y ou can see in the opening of the Jamal group two important features. First, and this is something I love, they have a sense of playfulness about their work. Do you notice the dreaming, the imagining that goes on? Sure it gets a little crazy, but in the work they want to accomplish, such playfulness is the heart of creativity! If I could go back and join in with them, I'd let it run a lot further than Dina is willing to let it go, though I think they need to think about some other things *before* the flight into fancy.

Second, these first minutes reveal a frightening trap that the committee just barely avoided. They nearly lost sight of their purpose in the first meeting, and if they hadn't been fortunate enough to slow down and articulate what they were all about, we wouldn't be reading about their work now. The surest way for any team to slip into oblivion is to fail in establishing purpose.

In my observations of middle school teams, I have rarely seen the members even *discuss* their purposes! There seems to be an unspoken agreement about why they are together, but I don't think it goes very far. If you were to ask most team members why they were together, you'd get fuzzy answers like these:

"Because teaming is the model for middle schools."

"My principal put us in teams."

"It's good for kids."

"It's the latest thing."

"It's the middle school philosophy."

These aren't purposes. If anything, they're excuses, apologies, and accidents. A few team members might speak of issues like the increased collegiality or support they receive, but again, this is probably a consequence of teaming rather than a purpose.

So what should be done? Just as the Jamal group had to dig around a bit before they came to agreement about their purpose, so should middle school teams discuss the reason they are together. There are many legitimate purposes for teaming at the middle school, and most of them complement one another. But no team will get anywhere until it takes on the task of defining its purpose. Does the team meet to support its members? Then that becomes the focus for its work. Does the team meet to improve student discipline? Fine. We understand this and we develop goals for our work based on this understanding. Many teams deal with the issue of creating interdisciplinary connections for their students. I'm afraid that they often do this in response to directives or vague guilt complexes. But if this is the purpose of the team, it becomes a possibility when the focus is defined.

Katzenbach and Smith (1993) anticipated the work of the Jamal group in their observations about teaming. They argue that "for a real team to form, there must be a team purpose that is distinctive and specific to the small group, and that requires its members to roll up their sleeves and work together to accomplish something beyond individual end-products" (pp. 242-3). In fact, their very definition of a team starts with the idea of purpose: "A team is a small number of people with comple-mentary skills who are committed to a common purpose, performance goals, and approach for which they hold themselves mutually accountable" (p. 45). Obviously, no middle school team will have success if it sees itself merely as an organizational convenience. Teaming for the sake of teaming makes no sense! Team for a reason.

What I would say the Jamal group teaches us most clearly in this opening section of the notes is that a team needs to discuss explicitly, openly, honestly, and whatever other -lys you want to add why it is together. From there, it is a small and logical step to establish some goals that the team can successfully achieve. Another anticipator of the Jamal study, J.R. Hackman (1990), saw the importance of this connection in his description of the *group spiral*. Basically, his point is that a group that starts off with some small successes will move toward success. A group that has initial failures will continue a downward spiral that is tough to reverse. By discussing purposes, the team can define what will count as the sort of success that starts the right spiral. If Thanksgiving comes around and you're not sure whether the team has been successful, it's probably because you didn't have the basis to decide. (Never mind if someone else – like your principal – sees success. You have to know!)

Maybe it's time to stop the study of the Jamal script and do some discussion. What is your team's purpose? No fair proceeding on assumptions, because you never know how your assumptions match those of your colleagues.

Here are a few ways you might use to come to some agreement about your purpose as a team. One, you might try writing an advertisement for a new team member. This doesn't mean you're kicking out one of your friends. It's a way of getting at what's important. Take a large sheet of paper and together construct an ad that indicates your team name, what you look for in team members, and most important, what your team is together to accomplish. (By the way, if you haven't got a team name, get one. It's clear from our experiences in sports and business that people can generate much more enthusiasm for an entity with an identity.) Through the act of putting your purpose into words, you can begin to build a commitment to this purpose. The Jamal group might have written an ad like this:

ADVERTISEMENT

When you look at the world, do you see what others miss?

When you imagine tomorrow, do you see better things than today?

THE JAMAL GROUP
is looking for someone who dreams of new worlds, someone who can listen to others and build on their ideas, someone who can help us create a new animal for a new world.

Join us!

As in so many cases, it's in the process of writing the ad rather than in the final product that the benefits appear. You'll arrive at some understanding of the kinds of qualities or behaviors your fellow teachers value. And you'll be pushed toward establishing a purpose that focuses your team and creates opportunities for success.

Another way to focus on your purpose is to build a team "charter," a practice that McIntosh-Fletcher (1996) recommends for business teams. I would modify her ideas slightly. (See Figure2, p. 14, to find the way I think a middle school team can think about its "charge" to team.) For now, though, following McIntosh-Fletcher's ideas, you could simply write a concise statement of purpose to include in the team charter. You can do this in relatively few words, but those words take on central importance in your team's direction. A third approach to understanding your own purpose builds on the work of another anticipator of the Jamal group's work. (It's interesting, by the way, that there appear to be more anticipators of this work in the world of business and organizational theory than there are in education. This example is one of the few in education.) In one study of the work of a middle school team over the course of a school year, Kain (1992) describes six purposes for teaming (modeled after McGrath, 1984). These are not meant to be the only purposes of teaming, but they do provide a starting point for the discussion. The purposes are pictured below:

Figure 1:
Team Purpose Circumplex

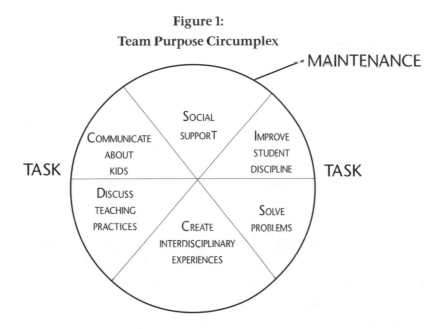

Which of these purposes does your team support and pursue? Which of these purposes do you feel your team should have as a priority? What purposes are not in the pie chart that you see as important to your work? How would you cut the pie differently? The purposes don't have to be seen as competing with one another, but it is nevertheless true that where you focus your energies, you'll find your successes. For example, if your team decides to make the creation of interdisciplinary experiences its focus for the year, it's likely that you will also experience some social support for team members and some discussion of teaching practices. But the center of your successes will be in the area of creating interdisciplinary experiences. Discussing your team's purpose openly and thoughtfully will help make the experience of teaming a meaningful one.

One distinction in the team circumplex pictured above is the difference between *task* and *maintenance*. This distinction was set out in Hoffman's (1982) work on problem solving in groups, and it offers a useful way of thinking for middle school teams. Some of the actions of a team are designed to accomplish specific tasks, such as building integrated curricula. Other team actions focus on creating a cohesive group that works well together, or *maintaining* the life of the group. In Hoffman's model, teams are always working at both levels, though only one is the explicit team focus at any given time.

What does this mean for middle school teams? For one thing, it reminds us that we need to consider both levels for our purpose focus. Attend to the well-being of the team, but don't neglect the tasks you set for yourselves.

Moving the purpose forward with goals

The Katzenbach and Smith (1993) definition of a team highlights a team's purpose, but the next part of the definition speaks of performance *goals*. A logical step to follow after agreeing on a team purpose is to translate that purpose into specific, achievable goals. I recommend that a team think about goals at three levels initially: a goal for next week, next month, and by the end of this term. These goals should be phrased in such a way that team members will definitely know whether the goals have been accomplished. Compare these goals: "By next week, we will reach all the kids on our team" *versus* "By next week, we will post the team theme in all of our rooms and explain it to each class." The former goal is vague and probably impossible; the latter is clear and easy to judge whether or not it has been achieved. I am not arguing for trivial goals, but for clarity.

Actually, more than clarity is important. The goals you set for your team should push you on that positive spiral I mentioned earlier (from Hackman, 1990). Set a goal that is worth accomplishing, but one that you can accomplish. Find and mark an early success for your team through the use of a clear goal. And when you accomplish next week's goal, set another for your team.

Take the time now to write goals for your team at the three levels I indicated. Make sure your goals fit the purpose you have articulated. The Jamal group focused its work by finding a purpose; they might have been even more effective if they had taken the next step and established their team goals.

A term used in the military to describe a serious threat to any operation is "mission creep." When a military group is sent somewhere to accomplish a specific purpose, but finds itself doing something else, it has fallen prey to "mission creep." For example, a group of marines sent to protect food shipments in April might find itself shoring up the government in August. Mission creep! The Jamal group was threatened with "mission creep" in this first discussion. If the team had not been able to bring focus to its work, it is unlikely we'd be studying their efforts today. And it's also a sad fact that the world might never have known the camel. *What might we – and the middle school students you face daily – be losing by your team's failure to establish a purpose?*

Figure 2: A "Charge" to Team at the Middle School

DATE:	TEAM NAME
Team members:	Subject/school position:
POSITION of team in school	
Team PURPOSE statement	
Team GOALS	
Team NORMS	
Team ACCOUNTABILITY PLAN	
Team REGULARITIES	

3.

"Does She Always Have to Have the Last Word?"

Developing Team Norms

The minutes

Dina: I think we probably ought to get going, don't you?

Melchuzar: Yes, but, I await the completion of our gathering.

Berodak: Sichem isn't here yet.

Dina: I know, but how long do we wait? We can help him catch up with us.

Berodak: I don't know.

Dina: Come on. Let's get at it.

Berodak: That really . . .

Dina: What?

Berodak: Nothing.

Melchuzar: Well, then. We were pretty clear about what our purpose would be at the last meeting: to design the beast of perfection for our people. Now, we just have to set out the features of this beast.

Rachel: I'm not sure we're ready for that. We started a list of functions for the beast, but—

Berodak: Excuse me, but we finished a list. As I recall, we spent a lot of time, way too much time on little details about this thing. I mean, who cares what color we choose?

Rachel: I don't think we chose a color.

Berodak: That's the point. Who cares. We can move on.

> What should they do about their tardy colleague? Is it important for a team to have an agreement about how they start their meetings?

Rachel: I don't agree. And maybe somebody does care. What arrogance! We need to go back and think about some of the important functions before we make too many decisions.

Berodak: Come on, Melchuzar. Does she have the right to control the whole group? Aren't you the leader? Let's get on with it.

Dina: I think you're being a little harsh on Rachel. It seems appropriate to open the discussion of functions now.

While we will examine the question of leadership later, watch for the challenge to Melchuzar's role in this section.

Melchuzar: But even as the oasis ends the journey, so the decision ends the discussion. We have a list, I believe.

Rachel: We don't! We only talked about transportation, and I'm thinking this beast could be useful to our people for food, too.

Berodak: So we'd eat our ticket out of here? Right. Why not make it a companion while we're at it. You could go for a ride, have a little conversation and a bite to eat all at once.

What does Berodak accomplish with his sarcasm? Humor has been proven to be a way to get more cohesion in a group. Teams need to be able to laugh together. But sarcasm is a risky, negative sort of humor, especially when it's directed at team members. Avoid it!

Rachel: Well, that's only an idea. My point is that it is worth going back now to look at some of our earlier ideas and add to them.

Berodak: And my point is that you aren't the only person here. Does she always have to have the last word? What gives her that power?

Rachel: Now hold on. I don't need to—

Melchuzar: Let's not get out of control. It's the cool breeze that softens the night.

Rachel: I'm not out of control, and you can blow your breeze right out—

Melchuzar: I'm sure I - What do you want?

Dina: Let's get some sort of agreement on our process. Can we go back to examine earlier decisions? Was there even a decision? Who's got the notes?

Melchuzar: Notes? What do you mean?

(Sichem noisily enters.)

Sichem:	Sorry I'm late. You wouldn't believe the crowds at the bazaar. Why I..
Dina:	Save it. We're in the middle of something.
Sichem:	Sorry.
Berodak:	It wasn't my idea to start without you.
Sichem:	It's okay.
Melchuzar:	As I was saying, what sort of notes?
Dina:	You mean no one has any record of what we did last time?
Berodak:	I certainly don't.
Rachel:	Not me.
Melchuzar:	No.
Sichem:	I don't even know what you're talking about.
Dina:	And weren't you all talking about writing scrolls and memoirs? Great. Now we have to back up.
Berodak:	Not necessarily. I remember it all. We agreed to a design of a small beast that could fly. It would be a very independent-minded animal. And, unlike other beasts, it would—
Rachel:	You don't know what *you're* talking about. What's this flying part?
Dina:	She's right, Berodak. And we've got to do something about what's going on in here, or else we'll just fight and never even know what we've done. People come in late...

WHOOPS! This happens all the time to teams. Some record of team discussions and decisions will prevent a lot of backtracking and pain.

Sichem:	I couldn't help it. And why couldn't you wait a minute?
Dina:	People working on unrelated business...
Melchuzar:	I have to have a total of my asses for the herdsmen. I'm still listening.
Berodak:	Can't they even count their own asses?
Dina:	People attacking other group members.
Berodak:	I didn't attack. I just asked a question.
Rachel:	Oh sure.
Dina:	No one with any idea of what we decided before.
Rachel:	I know.
Dina:	Or even how we decide something.
Rachel:	Well.
Dina:	Do you see what I mean? We've got to do something before we completely fall apart.
Melchuzar:	Once again, it seems that wisdom has spoken. May I suggest that we take on these issues now. Let us, even as the merchant lays his wares before the buyer, lay out how we shall work together.
Berodak:	Well, how can we? I mean, we don't know how we decide anything, so how can we decide to do that?
Dina:	Are you just mocking me?
Berodak:	No. I'm serious. We don't have the basis to decide how to decide.
Melchuzar:	Then let us agree now how we will make our decisions. What about complete agreement? Shall we agree that a decision is made when all of us agree to it? We talk it out until there is agreement, or there is no decision.
Dina:	That sounds workable.
Sichem:	But what if someone isn't here?
Rachel:	Try coming on time.
Sichem:	It's not just me.

Melchuzar:	True. Anyone might be gone at some time. Who can say where the wind next turns? But then, if we must wait, we may never finish our task.
Dina:	Who said to wait?
Melchuzar:	I assumed . . .
Dina:	That's part of the problem. Let's all stop assuming and talk about the very things we assume. If someone is not here, we just go on.
Rachel:	Sounds fair.
Berodak	I hate to miss one person's ideas.
Dina:	But can we ever get anywhere if we always are waiting on someone?
Sichem:	I was only late once!
Dina:	Not just you. It could be me.
Melchuzar:	Are we at least in agreement that we will make our decisions as a complete group? All of us decide or we haven't decided?
Rachel:	I thought we already decided that.
Berodak:	This is getting ridiculous.
Melchuzar:	Then let's decide it. Does anyone object? Good, then. So may it be written.
Sichem:	And just who is writing it?
Berodak:	Oh, no.

It's a powerful moment when a group decides to lay out assumptions for one another! This willingness to talk it through, to face the pain, promises success for a team.

Commentary

I t's a little distressing to examine this second sample from the records of the Jamal group. Their first meeting ended on a hopeful note: they had agreed upon a purpose for their work, and they had an enthusiasm for what they were about to do. The second gathering appears to be a disaster: Sichem is late and disruptive when he arrives, Rachel and Berodak have the beginnings of some pretty serious interpersonal conflict, Dina continues to threaten the leadership of Melchuzar, and Melchuzar actually works on a tally of his herds rather than focusing on the group's task. Take heart. We know they produced a camel!

What we're seeing clearly in this excerpt from the team's work is the development of what the team members value as important ways of acting and working together, or what psychologists call norms. And norms fit into a broader category of how groups work: the development of groups. We'll examine two issues based on this portion of the Jamal group minutes, team development and group norms.

Every team needs to realize that early in its team life, there is a crucial adjustment occurring at two levels. At one level, team members are adjusting to the social situation of being in a group: getting to know, respect, and tolerate other group members and the idea of being a part of a group. At another level, group members are getting accustomed to the idea of the task they need to perform. This is all a part of a group's forming (Tuckman, 1965), and it's not always easy.

Team development

Quite a few anticipators of the Jamal discovery have already described the ways in which teams develop or change over time. In fact, the research of these anticipators argues that it takes a lot of time for a team to get to be effective: from industry, we hear two to five years (Wellins, Byham, & Wilson, 1991), from middle schools, we hear one to three years (Erb & Doda, 1989). Most studies of team progress focus on what is different about various periods in the development of a team, and they call such differences "stages" or "phases" of development. For example, Wellins, Byham, and Wilson (1991), based on their work in the business world, describe four stages in team development. George (1982), working with middle school teams, has built a different four-stage model.

Figure 3: Comparison of Two-Stage Models of Team Development

WELLINS' STAGES	GEORGE'S STAGES
1. Getting started.	1. Organization.
2. Going in circles.	2. Community.
3. Getting on course.	3. Team teaching.
4. Full speed ahead.	4. Governmental.

But these are only two of many helpful ways of describing the development of teams or groups. The agreement of scholars is strong on one point: whether based on time, or focus, or precipitating events, teams do change over the course of their work.

Perhaps the most memorable scheme describing the changes groups go through was that written by the psychologist Bruce Tuckman (1965). Bringing together a great many research studies, he cleverly described a number of predictable stages that groups go through as indicated in Figure 4.

Figure 4: Tuckman's Stages of Group Development

Forming
Storming
Norming
Performing
Adjourning

First groups *form* by orienting themselves to one another and the tasks they face. Next, groups go through a period of *storming*, where group members resist the idea of becoming identified with a group and express hostility and resistance through their actions. The storming phase raises the issue of conflict, which can be an important aspect of a team's work together, but we'll deal with that more thoroughly in a later chapter. The third phase, *norming*, occurs as group members increasingly identify with the whole group and the tasks they face, creating a sense of cohesion. With this sense of cohesion, a typical group has established a social structure that supports the work they've set out to do and they do it. In this *perform-ing* stage, the group members become flexible about roles and quite focused on the task. A final stage in Tuckman's model is *adjourning,* which occurs once the task has been performed, although this applies less to the normal life of a middle school team.

What we see in this portion of the Jamal group records are elements of stages two and three: they start out storming (experiencing interpersonal conflict over how things get done, who does what, and so on) and begin the transition to norming (agreeing on what they value and how they will operate, which we hope will lead them to a sense of cohesion). Obviously there is no clear line between such stages, and some researchers challenge whether any distinguishable stages exist at all (Gersick, 1989). Still, there's something useful here for middle school team members to think about.

What does all this information about team development say to middle school teams? I see two very important lessons to focus on. First, whether you like the nautical analogy of Wellins et al. (1991), the poetic mnemonics of Tuckman (1965), the middle school stages of George (1982), or some other scheme, recognize that teams do develop. That is, a team just starting in August should look a lot different the following June (although it is possible to experience no development by ignor-ing a team). There are some ways to ensure that the change is positive (that's the point of this book!), but that the team will change is pretty much a given as long as the team does meet and attempt to do something. No team member should be discouraged about a momentary down time for the team, because the larger perspec-tive of team development offers a lot of hope.

The second lesson from all this work on team development is this: Teams should not sit back passively and wait for some sort of stage model to run over them (no one likes getting hit by a stage!). Instead, awareness of team development ought to push teams to take charge of the direction of the team. For example, if your team appears to be "going in circles," it does no good to do nothing and say, "well, that's just what happens with teaming. This too will pass." The greater understanding you now have should urge you to move the team further in its development, either through a discussion and analysis of why your team is stuck in an unproductive stage or through reaching out to an outsider who can help the team clarify why there is no forward progress.

An activity

In order to remove this discussion from the abstract level of group psychology, take a few moments with your team to start the following activity. Have each team member consider key events in your team life. Next, use the four boxes in Figure 5 to represent these events, either through drawings or brief descriptions. Based on the idea that teaming does evolve through stages, there are four unlabeled stages. Your job? Forget about what a researcher might have called them. Think of actual experiences or incidents you've had that would represent stages in your team's development. After you briefly describe or diagram these representative events, write a label for that stage. For example, you might have had a stormy session when your team tried to agree on classroom rules for all classes. You might symbolize this with dueling rulers and call this conflict stage "unruly rule-making." Choose something meaningful to you based on actual events in your team's life.

After each member has had time to focus individually on this task (I recommend a couple of days after), come together as a group to compare your results. Can you create a labeling scheme that has meaning for the whole team — taking bits and pieces from each others' ideas or creating new ideas based on your individual work? Where are you now? What is the next stage? And, perhaps most important of all, how will you get to that next level? The promise of this activity lies in each team member's individual reflections on teaming and the connections and discoveries teams can make when they open up discussion on the team's development.

Team norms

I started this chapter's commentary by defining *norms*, and now it's time to get back to that idea. Recall that norms are what the team members value as important ways of acting and working together. To be more formal, norms are "rules, implicit or explicit, established by groups to regulate the behavior of their members" (Johnson & Johnson, 1994, p. 20). Regulating behavior occurs by controlling the approval or rejection of group members' actions (Cummings, 1981). So, for example, the fact that Dina expressed her disapproval of Sichem's lateness, whereas many team members would politely ignore such behavior (or, more likely, talk about it when Sichem wasn't around!), begins to establish a norm for being on time, as well as a norm for expressing feelings about other group members' behavior. The way the Jamal members openly discuss whether or not it's okay to return to a previous decision forms the basis for a norm about the group process.

Figure 5
Stages in the evolution of the _____ Team

I _____	II _____
III _____	IV _____

Strange as it may seem, groups develop norms very quickly, sometimes in a few minutes and most often without ever actually discussing them (Ancona, 1990). Thus, norms remain powerful, but unspoken influences on how the group members will behave. In fact, even when faced with failure after failure, groups are unlikely to reexamine their norms (Cummings, 1981), and such unexamined norms can actually become powerful obstacles to team success (McIntosh-Fletcher, 1996). However, norms don't have to remain unspoken. A productive team activity is to open up group behavior for discussion. What should team meetings be like? What are the reasonable expectations team members bring with them?

For example, Sichem's lateness raises an important issue that all teams should address: what constitutes the beginning of a team meeting? I've watched many middle school teams begin in the most haphazard ways. The science teacher needs to grab a cup of coffee, the English teacher checks on the library schedule, the math teacher phones a parent, while the social studies teacher waits in her room for the team to gather. Fifteen minutes into the meeting time, everyone has gradually assembled, but there's frustration and a sense of wasted time. No one wants to criticize anyone else ("we're all professionals"), so the pattern continues. Only the next time, the social studies teacher decides to run to the media center, because the meeting won't start until fifteen minutes into the period. A norm has been established without speaking: "our meetings always start late." Whose fault is it? Everyone can blame someone else. But everyone begins to develop a sense of "how we do business."

Or consider Melchuzar's work on his donkey herds. He contends that he can listen effectively while totaling animals. After all, it's pretty mindless work. How often I've seen the same behavior in middle school team meetings! One teacher is readjusting seating charts; another teacher totals points to calculate midterm grades; one teacher marks assignments. A norm emerges: It's okay when we meet to give only part of our concentration to what we have to do (*in other words, it's not all that important*). Go ahead and conduct other business while we meet – if the meeting moves on to something really important to you, you can give it full attention. You can see this happen quite easily. The teacher who is totaling points sets aside his gradebook when he wants to advocate a new heading for the students' papers. The science teacher sets down her seating charts when the team starts to discuss adjusting the schedule for a lab activity.

The problem with that attitude, of course, is that it creates a fragmented collection of individuals, each with his or her own set of priorities, and no clear team focus. No matter how mindless the activity may seem, it distracts full attention from the team business, and it's probably going to have a powerful negative influence on the team's development. My recommendation to teams would be to forget about all that other stuff and focus on the business of the team itself, giving full attention to it. There are other opportunities for people to do the mindless, tedious activities that accompany teaching. (If God had not intended us to do mindless things, he never would have given us TV!) During the team meeting, listen actively, offer eye contact, and portray a commitment to what the team is all about.

Of course, there are many other norms that begin to surface in this meeting of the Jamal group. Rachel is accused of always having the last word (and this doesn't seem like a fair accusation to me). Who speaks at team meetings? That's an issue of norms. You've probably been in meetings where you wished so-and-so would just stop talking. And you've been in other meetings where you'd give anything to hear what so-and-so thinks. You've noticed that one person will interrupt some team members, but not others (Donnellon, 1996). Sometimes teams fall naturally into fair patterns of participation, and sometimes it takes strong leadership or the assistance of an outsider to quiet one member or draw out another. All that can be eased if a team addresses the issue explicitly, early in its team life.

On the other hand, norms are tricky because they can emerge in powerful ways despite your open discussions. I was in a school where the students and teacher in an advisory period were discussing the kinds of norms they wanted to establish for this unique class. The irony was that as the teacher was writing student suggestions like "listen to one another" on the board, students were rudely interrupting each other and forming small chat-groups that were totally ignoring the activity. What does this demonstrate? It's a lot easier to put norms on paper than it is to live them out. But it is inevitable that the norms will arise. In this advisory class, someone needed to confront openly those behaviors that were counter-productive before they became established norms. As I indicated earlier, it's a rare group that will go back and address the issue of norms, even though such a move is likely to help get more productive group behavior. Hackman and Morris (1975) suggest three ways to get groups to address norms: (a) diagnosis and feedback from one another concerning group norms, (b) process consultation from an outsider who observes a team's functioning, and (c) changing the nature of the task a group performs. Some of the activities below build on these ideas.

Norm activities

It's worth your time to pause again here and consider the norms of your team. I have a couple of suggestions to help you get at this.

First, try simply bringing the norms to a level of consciousness. As individual team members, make a list of "the way we do things around here." It's easy enough. You might start by jointly making a list of the way your faculty meetings run (you don't have to show this to the principal). How do meetings start? Who talks? How do decisions get made? What drives you nuts? (So-and-so always brings up his old school.) You get the idea. After building that list together so that everyone on the team agrees on the general task, independently build a similar list for your own team meetings. Bring your lists together so that you can openly discuss what kinds of behaviors you value as a team.

A caution: this is not meant to be a gripe session or an opportunity to put down your colleagues. Keep the discussion focused on what your meetings are like, with an eye to what an effective or ideal team meeting should be like. DO NOT accuse your colleagues of anything ("Well, if you weren't always late, Edna, we might have good meetings!"). You are aiming for common understanding and agreement on how the meetings are run and how you treat one another; you are not aiming at each other. Ultimately you want healthy norms, those that push you toward accomplishing your purposes. One important norm encouraged by this kind of activity is the willingness to discuss norms (Hackman & Oldham, 1980).

Go beyond merely listing the way business is conducted in your group. Using 3 X 5 cards, independently write down the kinds of norms you need to feel comfortable in the group (one norm per card). For example, you might write that you need meetings to start on time. This may or may not be important to the rest of the team. Then, take what each person has identified as personally important and construct a joint list of the essential operating norms. As a starting point, keep the list short – only items that you all agree on. You do not want to include items that the majority approve at the expense of the minority.

A second useful approach to this issue is to invite an outsider to one or two of your meetings with the specific purpose of listing what she sees as the norms of the group. Mind you, this is not an invitation to critique your team! This should be what is called a "clinical" observation. The outsider records what she sees happening as objectively as possible for the *team* to discuss. For example, she might simply tally up who talks in a given meeting or she might note the number of decisions made and who spoke for each. Unless you have a strong reason to do so, this should not be seen as an evaluation of the team (if your outsider is a "critical friend" all group members trust and respect, you might want more evaluative input). Indeed, a videotape of a couple of team meetings is closer to the kind of information your team wants here. Clearly, for this to be of any value at all, the team meeting should be "typical." That is, don't put on a show for the observer.

Once you have some observations recorded about the team's processes, use that information as the basis of a team discussion on the norms you've developed. The fundamental issue is this: which norms are contributing to your purpose and the optimal participation of each team member? and which norms are in need of re-examination? One point bears repeating. No team should say "we already did our norms" and grow complacent. Regularly take time to ask each other how the team process is working. Be ready to adjust to the needs you identify in such discussions.

You might now return to the Charge to Team (Figure 2) on p. 14 and list the team norms and regularities (where and when you meet, who takes on what responsibilities, who is leading, and so on). Your document should always be seen as a living document, something to change as the need arises. But as you articulate what your team stands for, you will find your team effectiveness continually improving.

Final comments

The discussion of group development should make it clear that it takes time to build teams (Maeroff, 1993; Dickinson & Erb, 1997). That's why it's not fair to make too much of the Jamal notes at the first of this chapter. A group of typical people can not become camel-makers without spending a lot of time learning to relate to one another and learning how to conduct their work. In your team efforts, you can become better camel-makers simply by opening up the neglected discussion of what your group values and how you would like to do business. Sometimes all that's needed is a window of opportunity, like the start of a new school year or semester, the addition of a team member, or even a simple entry point such as "I read an interesting idea yesterday. Maybe we should . . ."

4.

Melchuzar to the Rescue

Team Leadership

Note: It is clear from the following section of the minutes that some portions of the Jamal records have been left out. Space limitations demand this. I have, however, selected sections that provide the most useful and thought-provoking material for middle school teachers. — Dr. D

The minutes

Melchuzar: I am most pleased with our work. Though we have seen trying times and some difficulties, our progress is evident.

Berodak: I have to admit, that last discussion was worthwhile. Who would have thought about redesigning the hooves that way!

Dina: It was brilliant, Rachel. Feet that splay out to distribute the weight, soft, yet strong. They don't sink in loose sand.

Berodak: That thicker skin made a lot of sense. You know, you think about skin as skin, and it never really comes to mind that you can have ten times the thickness where it's needed! It's true that the sand is suited to the suppleness of skin rather than the hardness of hooves.

Dina: And the idea of rotating so that the foot stays in contact with the sand even longer. Excellent work. It's something no one would ever think of, and yet you pulled that idea out of the blue. Excellent.

Melchuzar: The richness of ideas exceeds the bounty of the dunes.

Dina: And there's no need to stop. What else shall we work on?

Berodak: Right. Any other thoughts, Rachel?

Rachel:	Well, I, I don't know. I guess I was thinking that maybe we ought to consider the motion again. I mean how it moves. My idea is, that, that …
Berodak:	Yes.
Rachel:	Well I guess, I'm thinking …
Sichem:	Here's my idea. I saw this animal once, and it was the most amazing thing.
Melchuzar:	Do you think Rachel was finished, Sichem?
Sichem:	Oh, sorry.
Rachel:	No, no. That's fine. What did you see?
Sichem:	This amazing animal like nothing you've ever seen. First, it was huge, but that's not what my idea is about. Its nose was like a snake, long and curved, but it moved like a snake, too. And it could grab things with this nose.
Dina:	Trunk.
Sichem:	I was not.
Dina:	No. That's what it's called, a trunk.
Sichem:	How do you know what I saw?
Berodak:	It's probably not what you saw, Sichem, but maybe she saw something like this.
Dina:	In fact, I did. And it's called an elephant.
Sichem:	So you know what it's called. You're missing my point. I think we need that.
Dina:	An elephant?
Sichem:	No. That kind of nose. It was incredible – and it makes the animal all that much more useful.
Rachel:	But I thought we already agreed that we wanted a noble head with a long, dignified snout.
Sichem:	They don't get any longer than this!
Rachel:	Dignified?

The praise they have for Rachel's work is fine. But notice the pressure put on her? It's enough to make someone reconsider making any more suggestions!

Sichem:	Who needs dignity when you can have practicality?
Dina:	Or absurdity.
Sichem:	Hey.
Dina:	I saw the elephant, and it's just not the kind of animal we're after. You can't believe how fat they are!
Sichem:	But if you saw one, with the trunk and all, you know how useful it is for the animal to have a nose that can grab things.
Melchuzar:	It is said that too long a nose invites the saber.
Rachel:	Huh?
Berodak:	Sichem might have a point. Why not use his idea? I mean, we've tried other people's ideas.
Rachel:	Because I'd rather not be laughed at when we get done with this project. Can you imagine taking this back, after all our work, and proudly handing it over to our people. "Here you are folks, your new horse with its own hookah!"
Berodak:	Seriously. There are times when an animal has to get food where it can. It's fine for your normal horse to graze along the grasses. But our horse won't have grasses all the time. It may very well need to eat at the leaves and branches it finds. I could see the value of such a nose to—
Rachel:	Call it a trunk if you must!
Berodak:	A trunk then. It's value is, you know, in that it can grab the branch, move it, you know. It reaches into places that would otherwise be impossible.
Sichem:	That's right. That's what I mean!
Rachel:	But you go back to the animal as it is, and our job is to design the perfect horse for our people. Not just another elephant!
Melchuzar:	Could it be that we could combine your ideas?
Sichem:	What do you mean?

Notice how Melchuzar is reducing conflict here but not attempting to cover over the disagreement? He's helping to keep the group focused in a way that doesn't harm any members.

Melchuzar:	Could it be that you, Sichem, might hear what Rachel says? That we do not need to copy the elephant?
Rachel:	Thank you.
Melchuzar:	And you, Rachel, could it be that you might probe the thoughts of Sichem without trampling them? Is it not true that he who finds the desert flower is best advised not to tread upon its stalk?
Rachel:	Huh?
Dina:	He has a point. If I'm getting this, Melchuzar, you're saying that there's something to what each one is saying.
Berodak:	That's what I heard.
Sichem:	But we are disagreeing! How do you find your flowers in that, Melchuzar?
Melchuzar:	Rachel has offered that this trunk would look foolish on our horse, but not that its usefulness is ridiculous. And you, Sichem, have put it to us that the trunk is useful, not beautiful. In fact, it's not the look of the thing that you care for. So let us keep the useful without marring our beauty.
Rachel:	But—
Berodak:	Let him finish.
Melchuzar:	We can build our horse's snout long *and* dignified, as we had hoped, but instead of placing a trunk at the end to dangle snake-like over the sands, we empower its lips with the same grasping power as the elephant's trunk.
Berodak:	Prehensile lips!
Sichem:	You don't have to get insulting.
Berodak:	No. That's the word – prehensile. They can grab things, operate independently. It's marvelous!
Dina:	Only not both. Why bother with this for the bottom lips? We keep them large and drooping, as befits a beast of burden. The upper lips we make prehensile, able to reach out.
Rachel:	And it doesn't have to look ridiculous?
Melchuzar:	Dignity, service, restraint.
Sichem:	But with agility too!

Melchuzar:	Agile as the breeze.
Rachel:	You have brought harmony, Melchuzar. We were right to choose you as our leader.
Berodak:	I don't remember choosing Melchuzar. No offense.
Sichem:	I don't either. Just why are you leader?
Melchuzar:	Surely, even as the dunes arise each in its appointed place and the seas find pathways to the shores, so the leader and the people walk together.
Dina:	Huh?
Rachel:	Huh?
Berodak:	Huh?
Sichem:	Huh?

Commentary

I promised a look at leadership, and it is coming. But first I need to point out a concept that applies to this entire study of the camel-makers. While there are elements of the minutes in this section that invite an exploration of the *topic* of leadership, it should be clear that the *issue* of leadership arises throughout the entire Jamal manuscript. Of course, that's no less true for issues like *norms* or *group processes* or *conflict* or anything else. In this regard, the Jamal notes are a perfect companion for a middle school team, because there is no issue in actual teaming that falls neatly and wholly into one compartment. **The effectiveness of teams is always determined by the continual interaction of a great many forces and influences.** Thus, when I focus commentary for this chapter on leadership, I hope my readers realize that that issue doesn't start and stop in these pages. Indeed, I invite the readers of the Jamal manuscript to probe the notes all the way through for any of the issues I raise anywhere in the commentary. That said, I do intend to deliver some commentary on the issue of leadership here. Early in the Jamal record, it became obvious that the leadership asserted by Melchuzar was not the heroic leadership implied by the title of this chapter: "Melchuzar to the Rescue!" even if he does a bit of rescuing here. I deliberately chose a dramatic title, to underscore the fact that many of us operate with some pretty inflated notions of what leadership means. As Peter Senge (1990) writes:

> *Especially in the West, leaders are heroes – great men (and occasionally women) who 'rise to the fore' in times of crises. Our prevailing leadership myths are still captured by the image of the captain of the cavalry leading the charge to rescue the settlers from the attacking Indians.* (p. 340)

Clearly, the leadership that Melchuzar represents, however flawed his practice may be, is not what has become the traditional (male?) domineering and heroic model of leadership. And I will argue that the leadership middle school teams require is also quite different from the "leader as hero." On the other hand, there is just as strong a tendency on such teams to conceive of the leader as some sort of clerk for the bureaucracy, which is no more helpful than hero models.

Quite a bit has been written about leadership, at the team level, the organizational level, even the national level. So, based on the Jamal experience, I ask myself what middle school teams need to know about leadership. I've decided to focus on just two questions that can help teams be better camel-makers:

- What understanding of leadership will improve team effectiveness?
- What can be done to increase leaders' effectiveness?

Leadership: honor or duty?

Not much evidence in the Jamal minutes could lead to the conclusion that Melchuzar occupies a position of high status because he is the leader. At the same time, it is not readily apparent that he performs any particularly unique tasks as leader. In fact, Melchuzar's leadership is sometimes disrespected, usurped, and ignored. Based on his example, what does leadership mean for a middle school team?

Researchers who anticipated the Jamal discovery have investigated the question of team leadership from quite a few different perspectives. Hackman and Walton (1986) write about the variety of approaches to understanding leadership: descriptive models of leaders' behavior; psychological theories of leaders' traits, styles, and charisma; social psychological theories about leaders' interactions with others; and theories designating how leaders ought to behave. Their own approach is to focus on leader functions in task-performing groups (Hackman & Walton, 1986, p. 73). This approach strikes me as productive. It seems that we can do more to enhance leadership if we think about *functions* and *processes* contributing to effectiveness than if we spend our efforts listing *traits* of greatness. If we get at what makes a Napoleon, for example, that probably won't take us far in making more Napoleons – even if that were desirable!

An examination of leader activities might help us understand how leadership has been conceptualized in middle school teams. The kinds of activities typically associated with leading a middle school team include the following: setting agendas, conducting team meetings, serving as liaison to the school administration, acting as spokesperson for the team, completing and coordinating lots of paperwork, and keeping records. If these are indeed typical – and a number of Jamal anticipators list them as such (Erb & Doda, 1989; Merenbloom, 1991; Porod, 1993; Whitford & Kyle, 1984) – then it would seem that being a leader at this level is embracing the duties of a clerkship rather than those of a visionary. Leadership would appear to be more duty than honor.

The notion of leadership expanded

Of course, focusing on activities is limited, too. One can be very active without being the least bit productive. Perhaps a way to bring all these activities together in a meaningful fashion is to place the idea of *purpose* back to the forefront (recall Chapter 2). Effective leaders are those who help teams achieve success, which means accomplishing some purpose. Leaders are neither heroes nor keepers of the bureaucratic red tape. Here's a continuum of the extreme views of leadership:

Leader as clerk:
files reports;
keeps records;
does the business of the school.

Leader as hero:
sets self apart;
comes in at end to set things right;
and brooks no dissent.

Leadership doesn't have to conform to one extreme or the other. Somewhere between those extremes is a version of leadership that involves moving a team toward success. An effective or successful team is one that accomplishes its purpose (or task), works together productively enough that team members would repeat the experience, and enhances the growth or other needs of its members (Hackman & Oldham, 1980). In the case of middle schools, does more learning occur in the teamed context? Success! Is the team experience positive for teachers? Success! Do teachers get better at their work through team activity? Success! A leader is committed to making that success happen, not to enhancing his or her own status or to carrying out the paper demands of the institution.

Increasing leader effectiveness

Leader selection. Let's set this concern aside quickly. We don't know exactly how Melchuzar came to be leader. Who appointed him? It doesn't matter. The strength of leadership does not come from some mandate or appointment ("I was appointed leader here and you better do what I say!"). Leadership strength comes from performance: helping the team produce and relate effectively. If you look at the leadership practices among teams beyond middle schools, you'll find that leaders attain their positions in a variety of ways. Sometimes leadership is rotated according to a schedule or individuals' expertise. An example of this was the Boeing team that developed the 777 aircraft. The leader for a given phase of the project was whoever had the necessary expertise (Fisher, 1993). Sometimes the leader is elected by other team members; sometimes the leader is appointed. Sometimes there isn't any official leader (Hirschhorn, 1991), but a sharing of leadership roles or the process of leadership (Dyer, 1995). It seems that any of these options is workable as long as the leader provides his or her team with three crucial functions: someone to hold the team to its purpose, someone to help establish and enforce productive norms, and someone to conduct the boundary business of the team.

Leader behaviors. *What should leaders do to be effective at making their teams effective?* The team's identity arises from commitment to a common purpose (go back to Chapter 2!). An effective leader helps the team establish and articulate that purpose. As the team works, it might sometimes wander from its purpose. Recall when the Jamal group lost sight of what it was attempting to do. An effective leader calls the team back to its purpose at that point. (By the way, was it Melchuzar who brought the team back? It need not be the "official" leader who exercises leadership!) Leadership means holding the team accountable for its purpose.

Just as purpose provides direction, norms and procedures provide the means to move in that direction. Effective leaders bring matters of values and processes to the level of conscious deliberation. That is, leaders encourage the sort of discussion that allows team members to express their feelings about their work together. Leaders remind the team of agreed-upon norms (such as "no grading papers during our meetings"). Leaders help their team members to think about how they do business and to modify unproductive patterns. It's no good accomplishing some noble purpose if team members are trampled in the process, and leaders can prevent such a trampling through careful attention to norms and values.

A final function of the leader is to help the team relate effectively to important persons, groups, and organizations outside of the team. This is the focus of Chapter 8, so I won't dwell on it here. However, no discussion of team leadership would be defensible without at least mentioning this crucial dimension of leadership. It is not necessary that the leader be the only one to relate to those outside the group (in fact, that's undesirable), but it is a necessary function of leadership to make sure the team attends to the external world.

It can be difficult to lead a team in a school structure, since teachers have long functioned under an assumption of equality of position. Still, a team without strong leadership is in danger. Here is a list of some actions to take and some to avoid in order to become an effective leader (from Kain, 1997b):

DO...................

- Help the team focus on a worthwhile purpose.
- Bring the group norms and procedures before the group.
- Actively connect your team to other forces in the school.
- Be an example of a team member willing to do your share of the work.
- View the highest accomplishment of leadership as opening opportunities for your colleagues.

DO NOT...................

- Blame team members.
- Excuse team members.
- Submit to "clerk" leadership, which attends only to paperwork.
- Fall into the "hero" model of leadership that sets you apart from your colleagues.

Rethinking leadership

Maybe thinking is not an "activity," but I propose that the best follow-up to the concepts in this chapter is to do some rethinking. Senge (1990) argues that "mental models" have a powerful effect on how we act. What mental models of leadership function in your team? Do you see leadership as a burdensome clerkship? a heroic act? a supportive coaching? shepherding? what? As members of your team, write the most appropriate metaphor for your team's version of leadership. Then discuss how the three crucial functions of leadership described in this chapter can best be fulfilled in your particular context. Also, consider how your team allows the leader to lead.

A word of caution. You may be well into the teaming experience and either disappointed with your leader or your own leadership. Remember that a lot of leaders get their positions without much training or support for leading. Don't hold yourself or others accountable for what you didn't know! And don't try to make too many changes at once. Melchuzar seems, in this section, to be getting better at leadership. That's a healthy perspective – getting better!

5.

"I've Got A Great Idea. We'll Use a Hump!"

Team Dialogues

The minutes

Berodak:	Can I make a suggestion for how we start today? We've really been putting off the most important problem we have to face, and I think it's because we're afraid of it. But we've got to deal with this some time; it might as well be now.
Sichem:	You mean ...
Rachel:	You know what he's getting at.
Sichem:	Commissions?
Dina:	Don't be ridiculous.
Melchuzar:	I think I can name this evil before you proceed. You're talking about ...
Berodak:	Right. Water.
Sichem:	Is that all? You had me a little nervous there. I'll get you some.
Berodak:	You don't understand.
Sichem:	I think I can handle this.
Dina:	No. He means for the horse.
Sichem:	So I'll get a bigger skin.
Berodak:	It's not a matter of watering a horse. It's a matter of water and the horse.
Sichem:	You lost me there.

40

Rachel: Berodak is raising a bigger issue, Sichem. He's saying there's a problem with the horse and the lack of water in the desert.

Sichem: Well, of course there is. That's a problem with everyone and everything that goes in the desert. It's just something we have to live with.

Dina: Maybe. But maybe not. If I hear what Berodak is not quite saying yet, he's suggesting that we ought to do something about the water problem inside of the horse.

So much depends on how we define the problems we deal with! Sometimes a team can really help here.

Sichem: That's ridiculous. The problem isn't inside the horse, it's inside the desert!

Berodak: Is it? I guess that's what I'm wondering about. We've had lots of wonderful ideas about this beast, but if we really want to design the beast of, of, what did you call it, Melchuzar?

Melchuzar: The beast of perfection. The glory of our people. The ...

Berodak: Close enough. The thing is, if we can't do something about this water problem, we won't get close to what Melchuzar is calling for.

Sichem: Well, we can't. That's obvious enough to anyone I think.

Rachel: That's a fairly close-minded approach to this, don't you think?

Sichem: Well, then, let's hear your idea!

Rachel: I, I, the thing is ...

Sichem: Case closed.

Melchuzar: Not too quickly. The absence of an idea is almost never permanent.

Sichem: But—

It may seem like Melchuzar is sounding like a politician here. But there's power in this idea: interacting ideas can bring new insight.

Melchuzar: Let us play with this idea first. Didn't Berodak simply say we hadn't yet faced the problem? He is reminding us of what we all should have seen anyway. Why should we be stopped for the simple lack of ideas?

Dina: Are you saying that having nothing to say shouldn't stop us from talking?

Melchuzar:	Not quite. I think I'm saying that the ideas we seek may await our speaking them out.
Rachel:	That sounds ridiculous! How can we speak out ideas we haven't had yet?
Melchuzar:	It may be that the idea is not within any one of us, but among us. And it awaits our speaking it into life.
Berodak:	You may be losing me, too, but I'm willing to try anyway. If I get you correctly, you're saying we can talk about this even though we don't know what we're talking about yet.
Melchuzar:	Exactly. We'll know what we think when we've said it.
Dina:	There's something there.
Berodak:	All right. The problem I'm talking about is water.
Sichem:	And unless you've got some idea for how to get more rain in the desert or a few more oases, I don't see what we can do.
Dina:	That's because you see the problem only one way. We've got to see it another way.
Sichem:	Such as?
Dina:	Well, I haven't worked that out yet.
Melchuzar:	But you have the start for us, and first steps on the journey make last steps smooth. It's how we see the problem. You've heard it before: give a man a fig, you feed him for a day; teach a man to fig, you feed him for a lifetime.
Rachel:	That needs work.
Melchuzar:	Maybe it's a date, not a fig. That matters no more than the shimmer of a palm branch. How can we see this problem differently?
Sichem:	Oh, I can do it. If we can't fix the problem of the water in the desert - and we can't! - we must fix the problem of the water in the horse.
Rachel:	So we need to get it to carry more water.
Dina:	If that's the issue, then we really do need to make larger horses, right? They have to carry more water, plus everything else we'll ask them to carry. Therefore, it seems logical that they are larger.
Berodak:	But if they are larger, then don't they need more water to survive? I mean, doesn't it cancel itself out? They carry more water, but since they are bigger, they consume more water?

Rachel: What if we design a system of water skins that conforms to the body of the horse?

Sichem: I don't follow you.

Rachel: What if the water skins were almost like another skin over the top of the horse? Then the water would be over the whole of the beast, so it not only carried more water, but the water it carried could cool its body and reduce the amount of water it needs?

Berodak: Brilliant. It wears its water! It's almost like the water is carried inside the horse!

Melchuzar: That's exactly the sort of thinking we need.

Dina: Wait a minute.

Melchuzar: But—

Dina: What did you say, Berodak?

Berodak: Brilliant?

Dina: No. After that.

Berodak: It's like carrying it in the horse?

Dina: That's it! Why not carry the water in the horse?

Rachel: Sounds disgusting.

Dina: I mean we could design a beast that stores its water differently from other animals.

Berodak: And uses its water more carefully so it has to store less.

Dina: All we need is some way to store the water. Maybe we could have some sort of hanging system, like the udders.

Sichem: You don't mean to leave those off, I hope.

Dina: No, like the udders, but different, too.

Sichem: Hey, I've got a great idea! We could use a hump!

Berodak: You're losing me, my friend.

Sichem: You know, the way the udders dangle under most animals? What if we sort of reverse this, put the udder on top! Only it's not an udder at all, but a bump, a sort of hump that stores all this extra water.

Dina: That's moving somewhere. A hump, huh?

Sichem:	Sure, and it would—
Rachel:	Slosh around, tip the animal over, make it impossible to carry anything at all, just for starters.
Sichem:	Well, it was just an idea.
Melchuzar:	And why do we abandon it so easily? Oases are too few to pass quickly by.
Dina:	Agreed. Who is to say this hump has to be a sloshing skin of water? Can't we do something else? Say, more fatty tissue to store the water. Then it would still respond like the flesh of any beast - no sloshing - but it would provide that extra bit of water.
Sichem:	That's a thought. But does fatty tissue solve the water problem?
Dina:	Not by itself. That's why we need more ideas.
Melchuzar:	Right. Let us explore some other approaches.

> It can be far too easy to do the nay-saying. Generate ideas first. Criticize later.

Commentary

For the record, it's important that my readers realize that the notes for this section end a bit too soon to see the complete development of the Jamal group's ideas. In fact, it is not the hump, but the camel's ability to reduce urine flow and absorb urea that makes it so efficient in water usage. But the Jamal discussions go on perhaps more than we need for the point of this section. It seems pretty clear to me that we can learn from what we've seen so far. And if I could reduce the lesson to a word, that word would be *dialogue*.

I'm made a bit nervous in using that word because it seems to be in vogue, and any time a word is in vogue one ought to be extra cautious about using it. A dialogue is currently the prescription for any societal ill, from sagging test scores to puffed up tax brackets. You could as easily encounter a suggestion for dialogue at a scholarly gathering as at a union meeting; you're as likely to hear it at a sporting event as at a hair dresser's. Got a problem? Dialogue! And that sort of popularity means we need to stand back from the word and explore it more carefully.

Senge (1990) credits David Bohm with making the crucial distinction between the ideas of dialogue and discussion. He begins by tracing the etymologies of those words. *Discussion* comes from the same root that gives us percussion and concussion, meaning a "striking," as in hammering your point home. *Dialogue* comes from words meaning "word through," or coming to something through words. Senge argues that teams need to learn to move back and forth between dialogue and discussion.

The richness of the word *dialogue* has been examined by the Russian linguist M. M. Bakhtin, who, though he lived before the discovery of the Jamal manuscript, would certainly have been a thoughtful commentator on the document. Bakhtin (1981) develops his understanding of *dialogue* in his discussion of the development of the novel. In particular, Bakhtin clarifies the way in which various languages interact with one another to create a novel. He doesn't mean languages like French and German and Tagalog; he means languages like the language of a social group or occupational community. Bakhtin argues that only in the interactions or *interanimation* of these different ways of speaking does each one reach its full potential.

Why the digression into Russian linguistics? There's an important lesson for middle school teams here. Dialogue is not the way we typically do business. In fact, the word *business* is especially important in this. When teams gather to do business, it becomes quite easy to reduce the quality of team interactions to those business items most easily addressed. It's far easier to discuss the business of a field trip than it is to discuss the idea of interconnections among subject areas; we'll talk about the business of managing a particular student's behavior more readily than the way mathematical thinking sheds new light on literature. The work of Bakhtin and others helps us understand how to move away from a view of meetings as business to a view of meetings as dialogue. Harvey and Drolet (1994) suggest a similar idea as a way of building teams: the "unmeeting." "You might try scheduling an 'unmeeting' in which team members just talk. Grand ideas emerge when people 'just talk'" (p. 37).

The Jamal members effectively construct a new kind of animal at least partially because they are willing to suspend typical committee business and to explore ideas. This is not without some pain and conflict, true, but the results are staggering. How can this example help teams become camel-makers?

A new way of viewing team meetings

Most teachers who have come to work on teaching teams have prior experiences that influence how we view team meetings. Before a teacher joined a dynamic, innovative team, it's likely he or she experienced countless committee meetings and more than a few faculty meetings. Neither one of these is a likely candidate for excitement and innovation. In fact, it's likely that the dominant impression teachers carry around regarding meetings is that they are a) too frequent, b) inefficient, c) unpleasant, and d) a waste of time. It's the view that a committee is "a group of people that keeps minutes and wastes hours." Given this perspective on meetings, it's easy to approach the team's meetings with more than a little suspicion and hostility. But teaming is not just another committee assignment. Teaming does not mean getting done with meetings so you can get back to the real world of teaching – it is the world of teaching. And unless we can approach team meetings with tolerance and the capacity to envisage a new kind of gathering, it's likely that team meetings will be no different from the inefficient, unpleasant, unproductive meetings we associate with committees.

Let me get practical. I have seen numerous teams who draw up agendas for their team meetings that focus almost exclusively on "business" issues. It's easy to discuss practical issues, like arranging buses for a field trip. And it's easy to discuss students – in fact, that topic could consume all of our team meeting time and more! When there isn't any actual "business" to discuss, such teams frequently don't even bother to meet. After all, there are plenty of tasks to be done if you're a teacher, and why should you waste time?

You shouldn't. That's a starting point. But what you consider to be a waste of time may deserve some scrutiny. Teachers, it seems, have a powerful ethic of practicality (Doyle & Ponder, 1977-1978). They want to spend their time – their limited, valuable time – on matters that influence their work quite directly. The problem is that it's not always clear what will impact one's work, and it's generally too easy to do the next thing that needs to be done. A fervent attention to the details of the immediate will almost guarantee that things go on as they have. It takes time and slow thoughtfulness to back away from the immediate concerns and re-think how things might need to change.

For middle school teachers who might be re-examining the way the curriculum has been "delivered" to students (in itself a metaphor worth re-examining!), the idea of dialogue is especially important. To build connections among the subject areas, or more importantly, to help students build connections among subject areas, teachers must reconceptualize their work. No longer are they "dispensers of information," loyal to the subject by their names or the textbook on the shelf. They are now *inquirers*, leading other inquirers. Dialogue is the proper posture of such inquirers.

Let me illustrate. One middle school team was meeting to deal with their weekly agenda. After they had "finished" the "business" of their meeting, the science teacher casually asked the English teacher what she was doing in class. She explained a visualization technique that struck a chord with the team's social studies teacher:

Catherine: I was having them imagine that they were blowing bubbles and that they, and, and some of them might have been imagining some pretty weird things. You know, it could be, because they were inside the bubble and they were going up and what could they see outside it and then they'd, they'd blow a really big bubble and then they were dribbling it and throwing it up into the basket and catching it. And, ah, then we talked afterwards about, you know, what things they'd seen... I was trying to get them to control their images, to be able to control the image. And it was just about a ten-minute exercise, fifteen minutes, but I had music playing and the room darkened down a bit and, and, ah you know, we just talked.

Trent:	You had them blowing bubbles?
Catherine:	But a lot of them are just, you know, treating it really, and I'm, and I'm trying to do various exercises with them so that they can realize that they do have a lot of images that they can draw on.
Trent:	That's neat. I can use that. I can build on that.
Catherine:	Can you?
Trent:	Because I've already talked about what history is, in fact is, is the use of the imagination to recreate the past.
Catherine:	Well would you build on that, Trent?
Trent:	Absolutely.
Catherine:	Because, I think that will be really important because some of these kids are just loving it and they're saying, 'When are we going to do this again?' . . .
Trent:	That lends itself perfectly to this project I'm working on. We're, we're, they're digging up hard data about a culture that existed 1500 years ago, and, once they've found that data, what are they going to do with it? And, I've told them the past is created, it is the use of the imagination. You take the facts, as you can find them, and then to communicate those facts to people, you have to create something with them. (Kain, 1992, pp. 196-197)

This example doesn't pretend to provide the key to integrated curricula. However, what's important here is that the interaction of ways of thinking about the world through the dialogue of team members helped each teacher re-think what his or her discipline was about. "Knowledge is generated anew from connections that weren't there before" (Wheately, 1992, p. 113). As James Beane has argued (1995a; 1997), the disciplines are not enemies to integration; indeed, they are indispensable allies. But the restricted versions of these disciplines that we tend to give our students in subject-specific classes are constricting and confusing.

HEAD IN THE CLOUDS ALERT! I realize this is all sounding a bit theoretical, and the Jamal notes have slipped into the background. So let me catch myself and focus on some practical matters for teams to think about. And if I'm to get practical, I might as well start numbering some ideas:

1. For teams, dialogue means that we can't merely conduct business (especially other people's business) at our meetings. It's unlikely that we'll ever talk about the ideas we deal with unless we consciously set out to do that – and that is dialogue.

2. Watch out for agendas. On the one hand, the agenda for team meetings is a wonderful ally, especially if it is democratically constructed. (I've seen some very effective teams take the first two minutes of each meeting to set the day's agenda, with everyone having a say in what the meeting will focus on.) On the other hand, the kinds of things we place on agendas tend to be more business-oriented than idea-oriented. Katzenbach and Smith (1993) observed that many good discussions have been cut short by arbitrary agendas. While they don't use the term *dialogue*, I think it's in keeping with their recommendations. They urge a continuous focus on the purpose of the team, something I think can be enhanced through dialogue. So the lesson is not to get rid of agendas, but to examine them and determine whether they seem trivial and arbitrary, whether they are keeping your team from the more important stuff.

3. Senge (1990) argues for a balance between the skills of inquiry and advocacy, a healthy way to keep perspective in team dialogues. Inquiry means looking into a matter, raising questions about it, challenging assumptions. Advocacy means supporting an idea, giving voice to it, energetically pushing for it. Neither of these positions is personal. As an inquirer, the English teacher questioning a plan or suggestion made by the science teacher is not attacking her personally. He is simply performing his duty, to help the team get the best possible results. We have a lot of baggage as team members: hurt feelings, insecurities, pride, jealousy (and some good things, too!). All too often, when we hear a question raised about our ideas, we direct it to some of that baggage rather than to the issue. Knowing about and talking about the roles of inquirer and advocate can help keep the focus on the generation of rich ideas.

4. Play. Melchuzar uses the phrase "let us play with this idea." That seems almost out of character for him, the business-like, serious Melchuzar. Yet he speaks wisdom in this sentence. To develop rich ideas in your teams and rich

ideas among your students, play is necessary. Play with words, play with ideas, even adopt a playful attitude about the team. Many of the outstanding examples of effective teams are characterized by this sort of playfulness (Katzenbach & Smith, 1993). The kind of rich dialogue that will lead to innovations in school that are as profound as the camel requires that we take our work seriously enough to have fun with it.

Humps

How about your team? How would you characterize the work you've done together? Has there been rich dialogue or business as usual for the school?

Try this activity. Take some of your old agendas or minutes from previous meetings. (If you have neither of those, at least try to think back on your meetings.) Using the headings as indicators of time, try to determine what percent of your time has been spent in the following kinds of activities: student discussion, red tape, scheduling matters, discipline, school issues, curriculum, and so on. What does this analysis tell you about your meetings?

Try having each team member (independently) identify what you could call your "hump," that is, some powerful and unique idea the group has developed together. Compare your answers. Maybe some team members are simply unaware of the accomplishments of the team. On the other hand, it may be that your team needs to change its approach a little, to make room for such ideas.

Finally, practice the roles of inquirer and advocate in your team. Actually do role-playing! One team member presents some idea for the team (for example, a plan to join curricula around the theme of work). The other team members practice inquiring into this idea. Have one team member stay out of the discussion to note ideas for feedback. As your team practices these roles, team members learn that they can mine ideas without scarring the source.

The Jamal team played with an idea long enough for it to pay off. It helped that they defined their task as a creative endeavor; it also helped that there were voices raised against the tendency to give up or simply accept things as they were. Middle school teams, too, can move toward camel-making. A key step is to re-think our meetings as *opportunities* to learn and create connections rather than *obligations* to fulfill.

6.

"That's Not the Way Horses Gallop!"

Freeing Teams from Constraints

The minutes

Rachel: I'd like to talk about the motion today.

Berodak: You mean?

Rachel: The way it moves.

Sichem: More feet stuff?

Rachel: No. I'm thinking about the bigger picture. Sort of putting it together and imagining how it will move.

Dina: That's a good idea, though maybe there's not too much reason to do so. Do we need to change that?

Sichem: Walking's walking, right?

Dina: I guess that's what I mean.

Berodak: Maybe. We could explore it a bit. What if we change the way it walks? There might be some advantages.

Sichem: But it could get silly, too. I mean we don't want to change everything. Some things are just the way they are.

Melchuzar: I do not know that we have ever lived with that credo.

Sichem: Well, really. What are you going to do with, say, nostrils? There's one for you: nostrils. You've got two holes for air. Should we make three?

Dina: There are other approaches. Maybe three's not the idea, but I bet we could come up with something useful if we worked at it.

Berodak: If we wanted to work at it.

Sichem:	Sure. How about this? The nostrils form a bag, like a leather wine skin, and they float above the animal to get out of the sand storms and retrieve fresh air!
Berodak:	I see it can get pretty silly.
Sichem:	Right.
Dina:	On the other hand, you've got something there.
Sichem:	What? I was being ridiculous.
Dina:	That's a real problem during the sand storms, breathing and all that. Never mind that the horse chokes immediately. Think about how long they are clogged with the sand afterwards and the damage to the lungs.
Berodak:	Maybe we should just get rid of the nostrils.
Melchuzar:	Or, perhaps, the nostrils ought to close. When the sands blow, you close your tent. Close the nostrils like the flap of a tent.
Sichem:	They would suffocate.
Melchuzar:	Obviously it can only be for a short time. Perhaps the worst blast of the storm. But there's something. The horse controls its nostrils, closing them when the sand is most furious.
Dina:	A great idea. We have to include it! It's true that you can rethink the most obvious, taken-for-granted things.
Sichem:	So much for my point.
Melchuzar:	We are grateful for your contributions, Sichem. Even in the midst of your jesting, we find treasures.
Berodak:	So, with newly flap-fitted nostrils, shall we go back to the issue of motion?
Rachel:	How about this, then? How about we have the legs on one side of body move together at the same time? Front and back on the left side together, then front and back on the right.
Sichem:	Like this? Oomph, oomph.
Melchuzar:	You make it look pretty comical, Sichem.
Sichem:	Watch the gallop!
Berodak:	That's not the way horses gallop!

Dina:	Well, we're in the business of designing something new, aren't we? I suppose we can change that, too.
Berodak:	I don't know. That's pretty serious.
Rachel:	I wasn't that serious about moving one side then the other. That was just an example.
Dina:	But there was nothing wrong with thinking about that and trying out the idea. I've learned that, at least, from our work together.
Melchuzar:	Indeed, that has proven true in our work.
Sichem:	So, what could be a reason for moving like that?
Dina:	Maybe something about the sand?
Berodak:	You know, thinking about it moving has raised a question in my mind. How do you get on the thing? It stands higher than the usual horse.
Melchuzar:	We could go back to a smaller animal. You're right about getting on the beast.
Dina:	But think about nostrils again. There may be another way.
Rachel:	Sure. We can have a contraption you climb on to mount the horse.
Sichem:	Then we'd have to, we'd have to take it everywhere. You can't take much else if you're always lugging around some sort of platform to mount the beast. Plus you'd have to have a way to haul it up after you used it to get up. Better to have some sort of dangling rope.
Dina:	A kind of mane perhaps? Really long and really strong. You grasp it to climb up onto the horse.
Berodak:	Or is this just a question of motion again?
Rachel:	How?
Berodak:	I mean, maybe its motion could help here. Say, it swoops low as it moves, so you can jump on. Sichem?
Sichem:	Right. Like this.
Rachel:	And then the rider just has to chase after it for a while, carrying whatever burdens, and leap to the horse's back.

Notice how one question leads to another and another. That's one of the wonderful things about working together.

Berodak:	That does sound a little funny.
Dina:	But swooping's not. Or at least, getting low. I was thinking how can we get the rider up high enough to mount the horse. Now I can see maybe we should think about getting the horse low enough.
Sichem:	Have it lie down?
Berodak:	It could never get up.
Dina:	Is there another option? Sichem, try lowering yourself without lying down.
Sichem:	I'm already on my knees.
Rachel:	There's a thought. If Sichem can be taught to go to his knees, then we ought to be able to teach the horse.
Sichem:	Thanks a lot.
Berodak:	Horses almost never go to their knees. If they do, well—
Dina:	Ah, but this is different. How about it? The horse goes down on its knees so that riders can climb aboard.
Sichem:	Then to get up it would have to . . . I'm not sure how it could get up.
Melchuzar:	Say it does so in pieces.
Sichem:	Whoa!
Melchuzar:	I mean one end at a time. The horse is resting with its legs tucked up under it.
Berodak:	It could develop some pretty major sores from that.
Dina:	Let him continue. I'm sure we can figure out a way to deal with the sores.

> It is interesting that the final design for the camel included leathery pads at key places to allow it to "couch." Some solutions generate other problems that need other creative solutions!

Melchuzar:	It thrusts its head forward to start the momentum, which allows it to get up to its knees. Then the hind quarters rise. We could have it bear most of its weight on the front end. The hind quarters rise together, then one at a time the front legs come up. It lifts its load or people in a series of motions.
Dina:	Sounds a little bumpy, but it could work.

Commentary

If one theme seems to emerge between the lines of this amazing Jamal document, it's this: putting together the creative power of a group of individuals can lead to great results. There are enough obstacles to success that it's not automatic and it is a lot of work. But what results!

A concept that has been beneath the surface throughout this examination of the Jamal document is "process losses" (Steiner, 1970). Basically, this idea says that if you have a group of people with a given amount of skill and resources, you should expect an amount of productivity equal to all the individual contributions combined. An equation might look like this:

$$\frac{individual\ talent\ and\ resources}{number\ of\ individuals} \times = productivity$$

The reality, in general, is that groups are not as productive as that formula suggests. Several people tugging on a rope do not produce the force that the same three people independently produce, even though the overall effect is significant. Process losses occur in the coordination of the individual efforts. Several people thinking through a problem may come up with better solutions than the individuals would have, but it takes care and coordination to make that happen.

Much of the commentary in this study is directed at minimizing the effects of such process losses. For example, establishing a clear purpose focuses the energy of team members to cut such losses. Developing and enforcing productive norms helps a team draw more from individual members. Handling conflict in positive ways (next chapter!) reduces the crippling effects conflict can produce without losing its potential for productive outcomes.

The focus of this chapter, however, is on an issue that rarely makes it into the works of Jamal anticipators. Process losses can be offset by the increase in creativity of a group, but only if that group is freed from the constraints of practice and tradition. This point is especially important for teachers. The socialization process teachers go through encourages a kind of independence from one another that is tough to break out of (Lortie, 1975).

Think about the creative ideas of the Jamal group. They devised an animal that adapted beautifully to the harsh desert environment. They managed to re-think the way it moved, the way it processed its fluids, the way it handled desert sand storms (nostrils that can close to keep out the blowing sands!), the way its feet coped with the sand, the sores it might develop from couching. One common thread through all these ideas is the importance of the team seeing its task as something new. They needed to realize that they could do things in a new way, that they could free themselves from constraints of tradition and establishment.

Teams of teachers at the middle school level are not merely a refinement for doing what we've always done. They may help in that, but that's simply too tame a goal. Businesses have done well with teams at that level. Here are some success stories:

- time to market for new products at Tektronix was cut from five years to eighteen months by an engineering team (Rayner, 1993).
- a cross-functional team at Enron (natural gas) streamlined construction processes, saving the company $10 million (Katzenbach & Smith, 1993).
- Hallmark cut the time needed to create new versions of cards from nine months to three months by reorganizing so that teams controlled the whole process (Grant, 1994).
- AT & T used cross-functional teams to produce the 4200 cordless phone in one-half the normal time, with lower costs and higher quality (Parker, 1994).
- a division of Kodak film used self-directed work teams to achieve the highest rating of production in the company's annual survey on quality of work life, while increasing output 12 percent and safety 67 percent, and decreasing costs by 11 percent (Fisher, 1993).
- cross functional teams at K Shoes saved the business! On-time delivery went from 80% to 97%; output per employee rose 19%, while labor costs went down 3%; and in terms of quality, rejects dropped from 5,000 parts per million to 250 parts per million (Wellins, Byham & Dixon, 1994).

While these are all powerful examples of improvements made through the team process, they don't highlight the truly substantial changes that might be made through that same process. Some companies, like Motorola and W.L. Gore, encourage teams to generate altogether new ideas. To get at that kind of creativity, let's look at a few of the constraints that teachers face and how we might free teachers from those constraints.

Egg-crate architecture

Many schools have a basic structural design that communicates a view of schooling as a series of separate activities that have nothing to do with one another. Each room is like the others, but each room is separate and isolated. Students roll egg-like from one room to the next where they settle into their neat rows for a brief period of time, often as passive as eggs in the refrigerator.

Teamed teachers more often than not inherit this architecture. It's not something that they can change. Just as the Jamal group found a new way of thinking about the problem of mounting the camel, teachers need to rethink how they might use their rooms to the students' advantage. Try tackling this issue as a team. Here are some questions to get you started:

- Do all students need to move from class to class daily? What are some other options, and what advantages and disadvantages do theses options entail? How can we re-think the use of space in our teaching?
- How might we re-configure student groups in order to reduce the impact of the architecture? (One team allowed students to pair up between math and English classes for a joint writing project to reduce the power of the barriers.)
- How can we get the students outside of the room structure for meaningful learning? Where else can we conduct learning on campus? Where can we encourage learning off campus? List some learning experiences that might allow your students to see themselves as a whole team rather than as a collection of classrooms.

What is important in this is that you begin to think like camel-makers. I've known some teams that used the school cafeteria creatively; I've known other teams that managed with a wide hallway. Your architecture limits what you can do? The architecture of the camel seemed to limit the Jamal group, but they freed themselves from the thinking that it had to be just another horse. Work to see your task as that sort of thinking.

Curriculum inflexibility

Another constraint middle school teachers complain about is the curriculum. "I'd love to work with my team to create integrated learning for my students, but I'm bound by the curriculum." In too many cases, this is true. There are expectations about what the students need to know for "next year;" there are problems generated by testing programs (Kain, 1997a). But the bindings may be a little more flexible than we think at first.

For example, if your curriculum requires that you teach some skill (such as map reading) to your students, it is likely that it does not specify exactly *how* you must teach that skill. Fortunately, we are not currently under the merciless rule of "teacher-proof" curricula. Teachers deserve the professional discretion to decide how best to accomplish the goals of the curriculum. There is the flexibility we need. Take charge of how you teach; don't let a textbook be the substitute teacher-proof curriculum. You may need to open a discussion of what's important to teach with colleagues at different grade levels. So much the better.

Of course, we might push this even further. As camel-makers, we could look to do something completely new. Mark Springer and Ed Silcox (Springer, 1994) demonstrate this kind of thinking in their organization of an entire school year around the exploration of a watershed. Students experience a completely different kind of schooling, without neglecting the skills and concepts that are most important to their education. They experience what John Lounsbury (in Springer) calls a freedom "from the traditional organizational barriers of subjects and schedules which often make education artificial and irrelevant" (p. ix).

A starting point to reach for such freedom might be for each team member to identify what are the central skills and concepts students need to learn (note: I deliberately used "learn" as opposed to what you need to teach; there are many ways to learn things). This is not an attempt to outline the content for a year, but a prioritizing exercise. What is central? Once you have identified these issues, make sure they aren't neglected. You can look for new ways to accomplish these goals, but don't let them slip.

Then, begin a dialogue with your team members about alternative ways to accomplish these goals. One promising approach to this is to conceive of the curriculum as an opportunity for students to solve problems. Savoie and Hughes (1994), for example, describe how they organized a two-week learning experience for their ninth graders around a family problem. Without diminishing the academic content, they report higher motivation among students. Students can attain academic goals in the solving of problems situated in real-world contexts, much as James Beane (1993; 1997) has called for in a curriculum that builds on problems and concerns of young adolescents. Problem-based learning becomes a powerful means of rethinking the curriculum constraint so that learning becomes more authentic (Glasgow, 1997; Stepien & Gallagher, 1993).

Another way of thinking about curriculum is to organize learning around curriculum blocks (Ahlgren & Kesidou, 1995). Based on the work of Project 2061, this notion arises from building scientific literacy throughout the K-12 experience. However, the new thinking represented in curriculum blocks provides another model for freeing ourselves from curricular constraints. Curriculum blocks are "coherent units of instruction that target a collection of benchmarks" (p. 45). Curriculum is organized around one of four purposes: description and explanation, problem solving, reflecting on issues, and inquiry. These curriculum blocks (an example is spending all day for a week designing a waste-disposal system for the cafeteria) provide a comprehensible unity for students. Thoughtful teams might rethink their curricula in terms of unifying blocks for the students, guided by benchmarks drawn from important concepts in their subject areas.

Of course, there are other models as well. Jacobs (1997) recommends mapping out the curriculum for a year to locate and/or create places where working together makes sense. Kain (1993) explains how teachers can find joint curriculum work in the intersection of the content of their subjects and the "intent" of their subjects' ways of thinking. The most important thing here is that teachers free themselves from the traditional and inflexible curriculum. "Too many teachers still act as if their job is to teach what they know or what is in the text, regardless of results. On the contrary, their job is to cause apt learnings and performance masteries to occur" (Wiggins, 1995, p. 118).

By thinking this way (i.e., to cause learning), teachers can find many ways to bring coherence and relevance to the students' experience. This "is not a search for a single, magical curriculum neatly bound in a three-ring binder or attractive textbook. Instead, it is a 'messy' exploration of the ways in which diverse people connect, organize, and make sense out of their experiences" (Beane, 1995b, p. 10). Team members need to be willing to shake off the way curriculum has always been and to enter the messiness with their colleagues. Team members need to move beyond the tyranny of covering some curriculum regardless of the learning that may or may not occur. Too often, the "curriculum" becomes an excuse for not working together as a team (Kain, 1997a). A word of caution. Sometimes surface changes in the curriculum deceive us. As Oakes, Vasudeva, and Jones (1996) discovered, the traditional ways of teaching, the traditional curriculum is powerful: "Nevertheless, the most salient finding from our interviews and observations is that traditional, teacher-directed instruction remains firmly in place in the vast majority of middle grades classes. Upon close inspection, we found that innovative-looking curriculum and learning activities often turned out to be conventional teacher-led, coverage-driven lessons" (p. 18).

Money

Teachers often avoid dealing with money issues. The budget appears to be a mystery, beyond their reach, fixed. Worse, the budget too often puts teachers in a position of beggars, grateful for any handout and fearful of pushing their benefactors' generosity too far. As a result, some of the potential for making changes or trying new things is lost.

The camel-makers faced similar "givens" with their "horse." "Walking is walking, right?" Wrong. Sometimes it is crucial to question the givens. One of the first givens to inquire into is the "mysterious" budget. If your team doesn't have a budget under its control, get one. You don't need a fortune; but the idea of controlling and spending money in ways you choose, without begging for alms is a new way of thinking that is long overdue.

Control over resources is an important element of empowerment. Fisher's (1993) acronym for successful empowerment of teams is ARIA: authority, *resources*, information, and accountability. Parker's (1994) definition of empowerment is similar: "Fully empowered teams are just that – they control their *resources*, set their goals, develop their plans, and then make and implement their decisions" (p. 74, emphasis added). Wellins et al. (1991) add that empowerment increases as responsibility increases. A new way of thinking for teams is to move away from the beggar mentality and seek control over some of the resources necessary to do their job. As Parker (1994) puts it, teams should not await empowerment as a gift, but must begin to act empowered to become empowered.

How would you spend money? Take some time now to list ways your team could productively control a budget. Think not only about what will help the students (materials, field trips, etc.), but also about what will help your team improve. Perhaps you would like to hire a consultant to assist you with a project or with your team processes. Perhaps you would like to fund the team's attendance at a conference or a retreat away from the work site. Perhaps you would like to start a team library of resources. By taking charge of a budget, your team begins to reconceptualize its position in the school. You can start to challenge some of the boundaries that have asserted themselves in your work.

Time

There are two levels to think about the issue of time. First, how does a team get enough time for team meetings? Second, how can the resource of time with students be used in new ways?

The biggest complaint teachers make about teaming is the time it demands. While there is no question that teaming is time-intensive, this can't become the excuse for allowing teams to fail to impact a school. Remind your administrators of the crucial importance of providing team time, as evidenced both in school experiences (Oakes et al., 1996; Strahan, Bowles, Richardson, & Hanawald, 1997) and business experiences (Wellins et al., 1994). Then, think creatively about what your team can do to get the time it needs. I've known numerous teams that have successfully asked for and received released time for the purposes of team planning. (If your administrator has seen you working hard, it's easier to convince him or her to grant you extra work time.) Other teams have convinced their administrators to use in-service time for team training (when businesses institute teaming, they generally provide weeks of training, with follow-up support for the first few years!) or other team activities. Another creative team bought time by juggling student groups during standardized testing. Some teams have met outside of school, though I see this as a short-term solution at best. Ideally, your team will have time built into the schedule to meet daily. However, just having a meeting time does not guarantee you will be able to use it well. In fact, there will be all sorts of issues crowding in on your meeting time, threatening what you want to accomplish.

Let me remind you of the importance of focusing on a team purpose. If this is not clearly established, your team meetings will wander off to other subjects, other concerns. If, for example, team meetings become rap sessions on what's wrong with the school or what's wrong with your current batch of students, of course you won't have the time you need. So don't let that happen. You will have more time if you keep the focus on your purpose. You will also have more time if you stick to your established process norms (things like starting on time) and if you maintain a strong system of informal communication. Take advantage of all the opportunities for interaction rather than meeting only formally.

As for the time constraints of the school schedule, these too are worth re-examining. Must learning experiences come in forty-seven minute parcels? Do the time slots have to be equal every day? Is there another way to think about time?

One of the few areas over which teachers have traditionally exercised tremendous control is their use of time. Just as the Jamal group manipulated its resources, your team can productively manipulate this valuable resource. For example, some teams have occasionally arranged for their students to spend the morning with just three of the teachers so that the fourth could use that time to seek materials. Other teams have extended lab periods or regrouped for videos so that time became available for individual teacher-student sessions or for teachers to plan. Begin to see time as flexible, something for you to use, rather than something that controls your team's potential.

Caution: self-imposed constraints

Especially as a group gets to be more cohesive, more like a family to the team members, a new risk arises. Concerned about maintaining smooth relationships, team members become more cautious, more conforming, more likely to erect what James Adams (1979) calls conceptual blocks. It is crucial that groups free themselves of the self-imposed constraint of affiliation: establish a tone that rewards members for wild ideas, new ways of seeing the world. Avoid the kind of pressure for consensus that threatens the generation of new ideas. Occasionally indulging in brainstorming or a technique like synectics (an activity to enhance creativity by making familiar ideas strange) can help your team keep a priority on creativity rather than conformity.

Here's a brainstorming task from Adams (1979) that provides a relevant exercise in thinking differently:

Invent (in reasonable detail) a better way to divide a large (2,000 sq. ft. or so) room into smaller spaces which can be used by various groups. This is an ongoing problem in schools. The dividing system should be flexible (space sizes easily changed), cheap, and aesthetically pleasing. (p. 137)

A similar brainstorming task would be to think of as many new ways as you can to use a set of four permanently divided rooms. Again, how could you change space sizes? How could flexibility be maintained? How could the four rooms be seen as team space vs. individual teachers' classrooms?

To apply the synectics technique, your team could begin with an analogy for what your students experience in the team context. Stretch that thinking by following the synectics process, which is presented in an easy-to-use version in Joyce and Weil (1992).

a) Create a series of analogies for the problem under consideration. What is being a student in our team like? (Example: a shopper at a crowded Walmart.)

b) Personalize the analogies for the problem under consideration. What does it feel like to be a shopping bag waiting to be filled? a cash register? and so on. (Example: nervous, empty, flimsy.)

c) Create compressed conflicts (oxymorons). From the words generated earlier, can you pair words that appear to fight with one another? (Example: a flimsy castle.)

d) Create a new analogy. What is like a "flimsy castle"? (Example: a snow fort.)

e) Return to the original problem. How can we apply the new analogy to our concern? (Example: Explain how being a student on our team is like living in a snow fort.)

In whatever thinking tasks your team takes on, the important point is to struggle against the kinds of constraints we build when we start to care about what others think of us. Nurture your team's creativity by indulging in wild thinking and expressing appreciation of team members who help push the team to be divergent.

Obviously, all these attempts to overturn constraints challenge some powerful traditions in schools, and the power of the institution in setting the conditions of teaming is significant (see Chapter 8). Perhaps the most important attitude to cultivate for a creative team that can be productive (overcome process losses) is the willingness to buck tradition. That means there will be the inevitable trauma of change, but there will also be the opportunity for camel making.

7.

"One Hump or Two?"

Conflict on Teams

The minutes

Dina:	You know, I had a thought. Maybe we ought to re-examine the idea of the hump. I've been thinking about how the horse looks, and how people might react to it. My concern is that this could create some problems.
Sichem:	Hey, the world's full of problems. Why just yesterday I—
Rachel:	Please, Sichem. Can't you be a little more serious about our work?
Sichem:	Ooh.
Rachel:	Just don't go on about this, please. I can't take it today.
Sichem:	Well, if that's the way you feel . . . sorry.
Dina:	Forget it, both of you. But what about the issue of looks?
Berodak:	For that matter, what about the issue of carrying loads? Just imagine trying to strap something onto the back of our horse! About the best you could do is balance a piece of straw on its back.
Rachel:	And that might break it!
Melchuzar:	It may be time to address such questions, but I would remind us all that there is danger in finding too many flaws in our work too soon. There are many ideas yet unspoken, and too soon is the knife to the fabric.
Dina:	Maybe. But maybe we will get off track if we don't take hard looks at what we've done. A critical eye, you know.
Rachel:	I agree with Dina. If we go on without exploring some of the consequences of our decisions, we could be creating some pretty big problems, problems that will make the rest of the work impossible.

Berodak:	Right. I mean, the feet are not a problem. That's settled.
Sichem:	Why that? If we have to look at everything, why not the feet?
Dina:	You seem to be taking this as a personal issue, Sichem, and it's not. The feet haven't come into question. It's not related to who suggested what.
Sichem:	That's easy enough for you to say now. But I think it is related to this. I mean, if I had suggested soft feet and Rachel had suggested the hump, we'd be talking about feet!
Berodak:	You're getting carried away, Sichem! How about a little detachment here? How about we get on the problem and off the personalities?
Sichem:	I just think it's unfair.
Rachel:	Maybe we ought to look at the feet then. I don't care.
Melchuzar:	Surely this is not just an issue of jealousy, is it? I cannot believe anyone here would be concerned about anything other than our horse and making it the best possible creature.
Sichem:	That's because you're . . .
Melchuzar:	What's that?
Sichem:	Forget it. Let's talk about the hump.
Dina:	The issue has two parts now, I think. First, the general appearance of the horse. It could be comical, maybe frightening. Second, Berodak's raised the issue of carrying loads.
Berodak:	Or people. How would you like to ride with that hump in your—
Dina:	So there are two issues.
Rachel:	What if we just re-think humps for a second.
Berodak:	Hump, you mean. It would get really ugly if we were talking about humps.

How hard it is NOT to take it personally when your ideas are challenged! Remember the roles of inquiry and advocacy?

Melchuzar exercises leadership here when he tries to bring the group back to purpose. He may be counterproductive in not taking the hurt feelings seriously enough.

Dina: Wait, though. Maybe that is part of the answer. At least for loads. What if you had two humps? There would be a sort of depression between them, and it would be easy to load up the animal that way.

Sichem: I can see that. We still get all the benefits of the hump, but then you do have a way to carry loads. Of course, we might be able to rig up some sort of device to put on the back of the horse to hold loads. It would be like a chest or something.

Rachel: So we ought to have a whole new hump design.

Sichem: That's not what I mean at all. You're only mocking me.

Rachel: Well, how would you like your horse, then?

Berodak: You mean one hump or two?

Sichem: That's it. I've taken all that I can stand. You make jokes at my expense, you laugh at my ideas. It's like you have your perfect little group, but I'm on the other side!

Berodak: Hold on, Sichem.

Sichem: Hold on, nothing. It's been one assault after another. I don't have to take this! Maybe you can just find another person to make the butt of your jokes.

Rachel: Aren't you taking this a little too seriously?

Sichem: I thought I was supposed to. I thought the whole problem here was I wouldn't be serious.

Melchuzar: I think it's time we talk not about the horse, but about us.

Commentary

onflict. You can see it in this section of the Jamal notes; you can see it in nearly *every* section of the Jamal notes. It's generally more of a problem between Sichem and Rachel than any other pair of the group, but it seems fairly widespread. Most often that conflict doesn't erupt into open hostility, as it does here. Still, there is that edge of conflict throughout. People always seem to find that one straw that breaks the camel's back.

What does it mean? Does the presence of conflict indicate there are problems that need to be solved? Does the group need a therapist? And what about teams in middle schools? Does conflict indicate a group is falling apart?

We'll look at the issue of conflict in this chapter, what it means and what might be done about it. But to start with, I want to make it clear that the fact that a group is experiencing conflict does not mean the group is dysfunctional or "at risk." In fact, if we are to believe what some important Jamal anticipators have to say, the absence of conflict might be a better indicator of trouble! Look at these ideas:

> *Teams that lack open conflict are dying entities.*
>
> (Harvey & Drolet,1994, p. 20)

> *[absence of conflict does not necessarily mean an effective team.] On the contrary, in my experience, one of the most reliable indicators of a team that is continually learning is the visible conflict of ideas.* (Senge 1990, p. 249)

> *Yet only when someone opens up a conflict - and one or more other people respond constructively - can individual differences and concerns be discussed and molded into common goals. Only then does the potential team give itself the chance to move ahead.* (Katzenbach and Smith, 1993, p. 111)

> *Resolving conflict should be viewed as positive, developmental, and a productive means to an end.* (Merenbloom, 1991, p. 101)

> *Conflict, either intrapersonal or interpersonal, is often the spark leading to creative thinking and creative actions . . . . Efforts to avoid or ignore conflict can have disastrous effects on group process and productivity. Groupthink may be*

viewed as one result of conflict avoidance. (Worchel, Coutant-Sassic, & Wong, 1993, p. 78, 80)

> *A healthy group does not suffer from a lack of conflict. Rather, the absence of conflict may signal apathy, disinterest, noninvolvement, and alienation – not maturity. In a healthy group, conflicts among members are inevitable.*
> (Johnson & Johnson, 1994, p. 294)

> *Conflict within a team is normal. In many ways, it's the life of a team.*
> (Douglass & Douglass, 1992, p. 17)

> *Conflict is a natural part of teamwork. In fact, attempts to avoid conflict can even backfire and cause more conflict. It is important, therefore, that team leaders, facilitators, and members deal with conflict in a healthy and constructive way. Some conflict can and should be avoided, while other conflict needs to be understood and resolved creatively. (McIntosh-Fletcher, 1996, p. 14)*

> *Get on with it, Drapolemac.* (Drapolemac's editor, 1998)

Of course, it would be taking things a bit to the extreme for your group deliberately to seek or manufacture conflict. It is, however, interesting that so much attention is given to *avoiding* conflict or resolving conflict, without recognizing that it can lead to some benefits. Among the chief benefits claimed for conflict are greater creativity (Johnson & Johnson, 1994), opportunities for growth (Harvey & Drolet, 1994), advanced warning of deeper troubles, and enhancement of diversity (Worchel, Coutant-Sassic & Wong, 1993). Still, all those benefits don't diminish the discomfort of conflict, and that will provide a focus for the commentary on the Jamal notes.

While I am inclined to agree with what the Jamal anticipators say about positive aspects of conflict, I also see that Sichem is quite uncomfortable in this portion of the group's work. I also recognize that a good many personal matters get mixed in with the group issues and the task the Jamal people have set for themselves. This uncomfortable, stressful, personally painful dimension of being on a team is not a slight matter. In fact, middle school teachers, accustomed to independent work, are more likely to back away from their commitments to the team – both at the emotional and the action levels – than to endure such discomfort. And, unfortunately, most of us are also more likely to deny or avoid the conflicts than to deal with them honestly.

What I propose is to examine four aspects of conflict with the theme of discomfort in mind. The four focal points are these: What *understanding* of conflict can help reduce this discomfort while enhancing the team's effectiveness? How can healthy *norms* on this issue help reduce the discomfort without merely glossing over conflict? How can *alignment* activities take the edge off conflict? What are some particularly useful *strategies* for dealing with conflict?

I do not think it's important that we reduce our team lives to predictable, trouble-free ventures. I like Wheatley's comment that as we progress "we stay comfortable with uncertainty, and confident of confusion's role" (1992, p. 151).

Understanding conflict

G. K. Chesterton once said that the chief goal of education is not to learn things, but to *unlearn* them. Our understanding of conflict needs some unlearning. As I've already indicated, the first unlearning we have to do relates to the negative feelings we associate with conflict. Conflict is an expected element of team life that promises growth, creativity, consideration of different points of view, better solutions, and as the Chinese curse puts it, "interesting" lives.

The most important understanding of conflict, then, is that it happens. Expect it. And when it does happen, don't assume your team is somehow sick or abnormal or ineffective. You may be on the edge of something great. You may be about to experience some very productive changes. You may also experience some hurt.

We can't downplay the risks of conflict. Katzenbach and Smith (1993), who praise the possibilities conflicts make possible, point out such risks: "Conflicts are risky – they can produce crippling animosities, hurt feelings, misunderstanding and disappointments" (p. 111). Therefore, a second understanding that is crucial to handling conflict is to know that conflict does inflict pain. Despite all our efforts to diminish this aspect of conflict, it remains. What team members must do is acknowledge that pain, and seek reconciliation.

At times, this pain can be inflicted without even realizing it, especially when team members come from diverse cultures. One example occurred on a team involving teachers from a variety of cultures. An English teacher asked the whole team if a certain night would work for a potluck dinner at her house. A consensus seemed to emerge, so she told everyone to come on Thursday. Later, one of her team members, a math teacher from Taiwan confronted this English teacher with, "We have to talk. Why are you angry with me?" The English teacher assured her she was not angry.

"Then why didn't you invite me to your dinner?" Apparently, the cultural norm she was accustomed to required a face-to-face, personal invitation. When the English teacher realized this, she was able to apologize and explain, and the hurt feelings were attended to.

Perhaps the key comes in that last statement: *feelings were attended to.* Attending to feelings of team members is central to handling conflict. It's crucial - especially during times of conflict - that team members invite each other to express feelings, even if members may be reluctant to do so at times. One middle school team developed a code for communicating that there were issues of hurt feelings that needed to be dealt with. Whenever a team member said "fried green tomatoes," that meant there was a feeling that needed to be dealt with, but later.

Jamal anticipators have helped clarify various types of conflict, which can be helpful in dealing with this issue. For example, Harvey and Drolet (1994, p. 80) describe five types of conflict: value, tangible, interpersonal, boundary, and perceptual conflicts. They maintain that handling conflict means first getting at the type of conflict in question.

At the middle school level, teams are more likely to see their conflicts falling into these categories: *philosophical* (like "value"), *interpersonal*, and *practical*. Philosophical conflicts occur when team members disagree on such issues as what counts for effective learning. One teacher believes that true learning occurs only when students encounter loosely structured problems and then seek resources and strategies to solve such problems, while another teacher believes students learn best in the repetition of basic skills on worksheets. The sort of conflict that results from these clashing positions is not easily resolved if the teachers are trying to work together to create learning experiences. To a certain extent, the skills of advocacy and inquiry (chapter five) and the "creative controversy" described below can help. However, such a conflict may be too great an obstacle, and the question is one of team composition rather than conflict resolution: maybe the team needs to be reconfigured when it can be done appropriately.

Interpersonal conflict generally concerns issues of style, "preferences" rather than "principles" (Harvey & Drolet, 1994). One teacher talks too much; another never arrives on time; a third has a tendency to gossip. I often hear teachers address the issue of personal compatibility as the linchpin of successful teaming. "We really like each other and get along well." The literature on teaming offers a contrasting viewpoint. Commitment and trust are necessary; personal friendships are not:

The evidence clearly is that teams whose members have a wide diversity of backgrounds, styles, and experiences have a greater opportunity to be more innovative, creative, and stimulating to other team members. Teams composed of people who are friends or who like one another may spend much of their time trying to keep the good feelings intact and may not be willing to face the disagreements, arguing, confrontation, hammering out of differences, or dealing with other issues that may be critical to productive problem solving or work.

(Dyer, 1995, pp. 21-22)

Katzenbach and Smith (1993) and Johnson and Johnson (1994) argue persuasively that teams should be composed of people with complementary skills rather than compatible personalities.

If teams are formed on the basis of complementary skills (and I'm aware that a lot of teams are formed for reasons that don't match the ideal), it's not surprising that there is interpersonal conflict. To minimize the discomfort of this sort of conflict, several understandings might be helpful.

First, keep the focus on what holds the team together: your purpose. A team that lacks a clear purpose can wallow in interpersonal muck because that emerges as the team's common, if unstable ground.

Second, extend grace to other team members. What seems tactless or inexplicable in another person may have a very good explanation, including the possibility of ignorance.

Third, if the problem is persistent and interfering with your team, talk about it. You may need to bring in an outsider for help on this, but don't let it fester. For example, I watched one team in action that suffered from the member who felt compelled to comment on everything. After anyone else spoke, she immediately commented. She finished her colleagues' sentences; she answered questions directed to others. In short, after about thirty minutes with her, other team members grew tense and irritable. One of the team members spoke with her about this situation, and in a very supportive manner, she offered to give her feedback about how often this woman was speaking. They worked out a code so that when the talkative teacher, who appeared to do her thinking aloud, spoke too much, her colleague gave her a visual sign. The plan brought a good deal of peace to the team.

The third kind of conflict I've seen among middle school teams is what I've called practical. That is, the conflict arises over day-to-day realities of practice. Personal issues are minimal, and for the most part, philosophical differences are not significant. Here's an example: a team decides to set common rules for all their students (a pretty helpful idea for the students who face arrays of rules!). One member wants no gum chewing, one member would rather ignore the issue, and two members don't care. This is not a problem of philosophy or personality. But it's important, both to the teacher who can't bear the chewing and the teacher who can't bear the idea of enforcing such a rule. Conflict results. Another example is the case where teachers want to agree on a common heading for their students' papers, but this leads to conflict. (One team spent two full days working out this particular problem.) Again, this is a question of practice, and conflict can and will arise in this context.

What is important in such practical conflicts is that the team again focus on its greater purpose – and here's a place where leadership can empower the whole group. If your team has decided to work on helping students connect their learning in an integrated fashion (i.e., this is your agreed-upon purpose), it is close to irrelevant whether or not they chew gum doing so. A better approach, perhaps, is to say it is irrelevant whether or not all team members agree on gum chewing. If one teacher can't live with the gum, so be it. This is the nature of practical conflicts. They tend to involve issues that take more work to get agreement on than they're worth. So the important understanding here is that if the conflict is practical in nature, teams should approach resolving such conflicts tolerantly: allow your colleagues to live with their preferences. When the conflict focuses on accomplishing your agreed upon purpose, try the constructive controversy approach outlined below.

A summary is in order. Understanding the type of conflict helps us know what to do. Philosophical conflict may be serious enough that you need to reconsider the composition of the team because this gets at the heart of your purpose in teaming. If your team is together for some specified period of time, work to generate ideas from your disagreements, but don't naively deny such philosophical differences. Interpersonal conflict arises from issues not directly related to your purpose. See the following section on norms, but recognize that interpersonal conflict can be diminished by focusing on your team's purpose. Finally, practical conflicts generally concern issues where the best practice is to offer latitude to your colleagues and to compromise as much as possible.

Beware of one dismal possibility. Johnston (1995) describes a team of teachers working on a discipline policy. The one dissenting member experienced stress and discomfort in his position, so he withdrew from the team. The conflict was solved, true, but the price was high: an important perspective was lost to the team. Kruse and Louis (1995) point out that the bonds developed by teacher teams resemble family bonds and that these bonds can become so important to the teachers that they simply will not risk bringing up issues of conflict. Other Jamal anticipators caution that "apparent peace should be recurrently examined" (Harvey & Drolet, 1995, p. 21). In contrast to the dominant view in schools, understand that a complete *absence* of conflict may indicate your team is in trouble. Think about that.

Norms on conflict

We already addressed the importance of establishing norms for the team's work together in Chapter 3. I don't want to repeat that material, but the area of conflict is one that requires special care in this regard and is worth a special section in this chapter. The typical norm for teams' dealing with conflict involves feeling hurt, angry, or frustrated, denying one's feelings to those persons most directly concerned, and then expressing them in an inappropriate context. Sichem gets angry at Rachel, but instead of saying so to her, he pretends everything is fine. Later he finds Berodak to complain, "Can you believe how arrogant Rachel is? Did you hear what she said?" Now he has not only deceived Rachel and erected barriers between the two of them, but he has also damaged Rachel's reputation with Berodak. The effect snowballs.

Teams often avoid addressing the issue of conflict in their initial norming because to do so seems to invite disaster. Why should we set ourselves up for failure? they ask. It's like a couple entering a marriage with an agreement drawn up about how they will divide their possessions when they split up - not exactly a promising start! However, given what we know about teaming, that conflict can be expected and can be productive, it is shortsighted for teams to avoid this issue in their "norming" stage.

Here's an example of a team that avoided setting norms about conflict. The social studies teacher had a particularly unproductive practice. At team parent conferences, he would frequently make a comment like this: "I don't know what all the fuss is about. I never have any trouble with Louie." The other three teachers inevitably felt put down by this sort of comment. But no one on the team confronted this particular teacher. ("After all, we're professionals.") Instead, they grumbled to one another and other teachers and allowed a resentment to build against their colleague. The team gave every appearance of a cohesive, non-conflicting group, but something was seething underneath, and a one-upmanship in parent conferencing emerged.

This particular team didn't explicitly address the issue of norms, and it certainly avoided the topic of conflict. What I'd like to argue for, though, is a willingness of teams to take on conflict before conflict takes them on. Here are some simple things you can do within your team to establish healthy norms about conflict:

- **Talk through the issue of conflict in an early norm-setting meeting.** Specifically, allow members to express how they feel about conflictual situations and what would help to diminish the discomfort they experience without denying the basic conflict. Be aware that people do have differing comfort levels about being confronted and confronting others.

- **Have each team member express a way in which other people have successfully conflicted with him or her.** In other words, how have others been able to oppose you without alienating you? From this discussion, compile a list of positive ways to confront one another.

- **Follow up your norm-setting with a role-play on conflict.** Apply the processes you've agreed upon for this; have at least one member observe and comment on how the conflict was handled. Here are some conflicting positions you could use (or create your own):

    Person One: You have been expecting your colleague to provide a list of activities for a unit your team agreed on several weeks ago. The deadline was your last team meeting, but your colleague did not have the list ready then. No one on the team seemed upset about this—in fact, the excuse seemed reasonable. It's now a week later, and when you ask about the materials, you get another excuse. You are frustrated that no one else on the team seems to worry about this, and if you say anything, you'll be the "bad guy." Confront your colleague.

    Person Two: You were supposed to have a list of activities for a new unit ready to give your team members at this meeting. But you've been busy. The duties of coaching and teaching keep getting in the way. You expect your team members to be understanding and tolerant. After all, you've cut them slack on more than one occasion. One colleague, however, is particularly upset about this issue and lets you know it. You think it's unfair and appeal to other team members for support.

- If your team finds conflict too uncomfortable to deal with immediately, develop a code like the team featured earlier in this chapter ("fried green tomatoes"). Establish the ground rule that the use of the code means a team member is free to pull back from an issue until the next meeting (or a one-on-one direct confrontation), at which time he or she will honestly address the conflict in question.

- **Periodically discuss the role of conflict in your team.** Pay particular attention to the possibility that you might be avoiding or denying problems. Senge (1990) talks about "defensive routines" people use to avoid the hurt associated with conflict. Defensive routines are "entrenched habits we use to protect ourselves from the embarrassment and threat that come with exposing our thinking. Defensive routines form a sort of protective shell around our deepest assumptions, defending us against pain, but also keeping us from learning about the causes of the pain" (p. 250). Senge points out that the power of these routines lies in their hiddenness – as soon as we discuss them, they lose their power. Make it a regular practice of your team to check in on team members' feelings about your task and your group processes. Share the responsibility of probing members and bringing defensive routines to light.

The key thing to remember about norming is that it happens one way or another. It's likely that unproductive norms for dealing with conflict will emerge and dominate your team unless your team discusses and agrees on some productive ones. Also, don't naïvely believe that you've already "done" norming. Revisiting norms is a healthy practice throughout the life of your team.

Alignment of the team

Another way to take some of the discomfort out of conflict is to spend time in an alignment activity. Culbert and McDonough (1980) argue that one reason there is so much discomfort in the world of work is that people have to disguise and deny their self-interests. However, this isn't necessary. Good alignment occurs when the core values that give meaning to an individual's life are brought into the work world, allowing him or her to contribute to the success of the organization (Culbert & McDonough, 1980, pp. 60-61).

At a team level, this relates to the expectations team members have of one another. If I know, for example, that my teammate's long-term goal is to become a principal and that she is enrolled in a college course, I can understand why she doesn't want to commit to a project that might take all of her spare time. If I know that another team member's most admired person was a philosopher, I can understand better why he likes to engage in what seem to me like drawn-out, abstract conversations. The point is that by understanding what motivates and moves another person, I am better able to adjust my expectations of that person. In doing so, I reduce the frustrations and disappointments that false expectations set me up for (Dyer, 1995).

Mitchell (1986) tested alignment activities for team-building and found them to be helpful in teams' accomplishing their purposes. Essentially, the process consists of a) having individuals answer a set of questions about themselves, their career interests, and their current job; b) sharing answers in a round-robin fashion; and c) as a group, processing feelings and insights from this sharing. It can be helpful to have more information presented about alignment to begin with, but I've found the act of addressing alignment questions to be quite successful in itself for helping team members develop realistic expectations. It also makes a good way to get to know one another early on in the team's life.

Here's a set of questions modeled after Mitchell's work. Try spending an early meeting in alignment activities.

1. How would you like to be remembered by others?
2. In what ways are you most often misunderstood by others?
3. Who are some important role models in your life?
4. What would you most like to accomplish in your preferred career (either where you are now or where you would like to be)?
5. If you could customize your work role on this team, what would the role look like?
6. In relation to this team, what word or phrase would you use to describe a) you, b) you as others see you, c) you as you would like to be seen?
7. What is the next lesson you need to learn in your work and what are your plans for doing so?

Strategies

Finally, I'll list several strategies your team, or a small group of teams, can try in order to deal with some of the discomfort associated with conflict. Johnson and Johnson (1994, pp. 290-293) use conflict in a powerful, systematic structure to turn controversy into creativity. Their procedure involves subgroups taking contrasting positions on particular issues. This systematically allows the team to explore all aspects of a controversy. The steps of their process are as follows:

1. Members of subgroups are assigned positions on a controversial topic to advocate. Their personal feelings are not at issue. For example, I might be given the task of arguing for including the art teacher on our team, even though I oppose this idea.
2. Each advocacy group presents its ideas to the team as persuasively as possible. Others listen critically in order to conflict with that group's position. This leads to a general discussion that is likely to induce uncertainty among team members.
3. Based on this uncertainty, members seek more information, and they seek to understand the rationale of the opposing position.
4. Group members reverse positions. Subgroups are asked to present the opposing position as forcefully and persuasively as possible.
5. The group works for consensus based on all the ideas that have emerged in the process.

This particular technique guarantees that issues will be explored in depth and that all members will be encouraged to explore multiple perspectives. It reduces the "personal" nature of controversy, establishing a problem-solving tone for the team. Discomfort is reduced by the detached exploration of problems.

A second strategy for dealing with conflict is to use outsiders. Occasionally, it becomes clear that a team needs help in easing conflictual situations. I addressed this issue in Chapter 3, but to remind you, there are times when an outsider's view can help to strip away some of the blinders we acquire in our work. As an "objective" observer, the outsider can describe what he or she sees happening in the conflict. Team members can be invited to discuss openly the nature of the conflict in the presence of this outsider who asks clarifying questions. For example, this outsider might help team members clarify what they expect from one another and where offense is being given. The outsider can assist in clarifying the roles different members assume. Also, the outsider can provide feedback, such as who is talking during meetings, to help the team see its ways of functioning. It is unfair to expect the outsider to become an arbiter of conflict; rather this person can facilitate the team's ability to solve its own conflicts.

Conflict needs to assume its rightful role in our teams. It can generate some positive results as long as we deal with it properly. The risk of avoiding conflict is simply too great: "Teachers unwilling to deal directly with conflict strike compromises instead. . . . Team members end up trading comfort for critical analysis of their work" (Kruse & Louis, 1995, p. 6).

8.

"They're Laughing at Our Horse!"

Teams and Boundary Relations

The minutes

Berodak:	I hate to have to start us off today with bad news, but I've got some.
Dina:	I knew it.
Sichem:	It's the hump, isn't it?
Berodak:	Actually, the problem is more related to—
Rachel:	The feet? Oh, I thought that would be the one area where we'd be able to stick to our position.
Berodak:	Not the feet. It's—
Sichem:	Please don't say the nose. That was just too much work.
Dina:	Maybe we ought to let him finish!
Melchuzar:	Excellent idea. The man can't get a word out. We're all awaiting the news he brings, yet one after another we continue our speculations. The pool is deep, as the saying goes, but only a few may drink at once. If we—
Dina:	Melchuzar.
Melchuzar:	Yes.
Dina:	Let him talk.
Melchuzar:	Right you are.
Berodak:	Well, I was on my way here, just taking my time because I knew I'd be here early, but not knowing what I'd run into. You know the drawing we put together of our ideas so far? I thought that was here somewhere, because I wasn't able to find it at home.
Sichem:	You lost our drawing?

Berodak:	Hear me out. I thought it was here, but then as I was walking through the bazaar, I saw a group of people clustered about one man, and they were laughing riotously. I am, as you know, a sociable fellow, and I thought I'd only just stop a moment to join in with their levity. What should I see in their midst but the drawing of our horse!
Dina:	How could they have it? We weren't going to tell anyone yet!
Berodak:	Believe me, no one could have been more surprised than I. But there they were laughing. I thought I'd learn their joke, but soon realized that there was no joke. Only the picture. They were laughing at our horse!
Sichem:	But why?
Dina:	Well, it does look a bit odd, you have to admit.
Sichem:	The nose, probably.
Rachel:	Or the hump!
Melchuzar:	No point in fighting. Are you sure, Berodak, are you sure they were laughing at the horse we've designed?
Berodak:	Absolutely. I'd like to be able to tell a story or recount some absurdity. But the fact is, I saw them gathered in a cluster, shaking with laughter at the picture before them. "Look at that back!" one cried, "what a deformity." "The fabled mountain of Melchuzar," said another. Naturally, I didn't claim to have anything to do with the picture. I feel proud of our work, really, and I'm glad to work with all of you. But, hey, they're laughing at our horse!
Melchuzar:	Huh. I have no words.
Sichem:	Unbelievable.
Dina:	It's terrible.
Berodak:	Or worse.
Rachel:	It's like being kicked, isn't it?
Berodak:	Or worse. What do we do now? I mean we can't go on. It would be a complete waste of time.
Melchuzar:	You can't mean . . .
Berodak:	Of course I can! We're done!
Dina:	I don't think so, though I'm not sure what we should do yet. But we can't just stop because a few people laugh.

Berodak: Look, those are the people we wanted to help. Not much chance of that now. And it's not like a few people laughing. Practically a mob in hysterics.

Dina: But what if we go out and talk to them. I mean, what if, instead of just looking at the drawing and laughing, they listen to our ideas and all the things they can gain from the horse.

Sichem: Sounds like fun. Especially if you like the idea of being stoned.

> There's a temptation to give up at this sort of obstacle. Teams have to be careful not to react too dramatically to criticism. There will be those just waiting for your failures.

Melchuzar: Wait. Dina's words are again full of wisdom. It seems we have two paths before us. One leads us back to the starting point and beyond, ending our work on this altogether. The other leads us right into the bazaar, surrounded by the laughter and mockery, struggling to win back our dignity, stretched and humiliated, perhaps, but continuing with what we set out to do. Let us not forget when we finally came to our agreement that we would create the beast of perfection. Why stop now?

> Three cheers for leadership!

Rachel: I'm with you Melchuzar, but I can't help feeling this all came about because someone wasn't very careful with the drawing.

Berodak: Hey!

Sichem: Well she's right, Berodak. It's no good making excuses. You took it, you left it somewhere, and now we all pay the price.

Melchuzar: It's also no good, as you say, dwelling on this. The question now is what can we do to win back the trust and support of the crowd in the bazaar.

Dina: Right. Perhaps the problem goes beyond the lost picture. Maybe we made a mistake a long time ago when we failed to inform the so-called "mob" of what we were trying to do.

Melchuzar: It would seem that these are true words, too. Strange, isn't it? At the time, our only concern was getting started on the design, exploring countless possibilities, dreaming aloud. But I can see now, as one sees at the rise of the great dunes, where our turning was misguided.

Rachel: So who has an idea of what we should do now?

Commentary

The Jamal group faces a problem that many teams at the middle school experience. Just when the team finally seems to have resolved its internal problems and begun to enjoy success, Berodak brings the bad news that others do not like what they're doing. Hurt feelings aside, this represents a serious problem for the work of this team, but a problem they can address productively. And it represents an area that has been neglected far too often among otherwise successful teams: *boundary issues.*

Figure 5

Team relating to those outside of team boundary

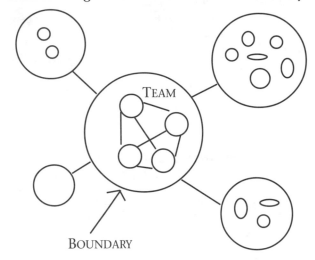

Why boundaries?

Most of the literature about teaming focuses on how teams accomplish their tasks (whatever work they set out to do) or how they maintain good working relations within the team (team-building or conflict resolution, for example). In both cases, the focus is inside the boundary in the above diagram. Boundary issues concern the active attempts on the part of a team to relate effectively to other persons, groups, and organizations. What ways does the team mark itself as different or separate from other teams (boundary maintenance)? And what ways does the team establish relationships, share information, join with others (boundary spanning)?

Concern for the group boundaries tends to be one of the last things a group worries about. The thinking seems to go something like this: "Begin to create a cohesive group and get started on the work that has to be done; then relating to others will take care of itself when it has to." There are several reasons why this line of reasoning deserves careful examination.

First, if teams put off boundary considerations too long, they may find that they can't deal with others in any new ways. Patterns have been established; attitudes have been set; first impressions have, as they so often do, hardened into unchange-able perceptions. "Since an environment changes whispers into roars, teams must manage the information and images they send out. These images appear to get cast in concrete..." (Ancona, 1990, p. 358). You can see this in the trouble facing the Jamal group. Their task is not the relatively simple one of presenting themselves and their work as something new to the public; due to their delay, their task has become the complicated and difficult work of *changing* established opinions and perceptions.

Also, by putting off boundary considerations teams may miss the valuable input of outsiders. Not only has the team's capacity to influence others been neutralized, but the possibility for others to influence the team may have diminished or disappeared. Those same people laughing at Berodak's misplaced drawing, if involved more carefully and sooner, might have helped to sculpt the camel rather than huddled to scorn it.

Third, and this is probably the most important issue, by avoiding the question of boundary issues, teams may seriously undermine their success in accomplishing the task they have set out on. I'm not simply saying they miss outsiders' input; focusing inward and avoiding boundary issues may actually reduce the team's potential for success (Ancona, 1990; Maeroff, 1993). In other words, rather than focusing inward so that they can develop the cohesiveness to present a better front to the rest of the world, by focusing inward the team becomes *less* cohesive, *less* successful.

Finally, it is important for teams to conceive of their success as the success of the school. A highly successful team will not make much difference if the whole school is unaffected. Teams need to relate to one another. As one teacher put it, "Years ago we had teacher isolation, and then once we reorganized, we had team isolation" (Kruse & Louis, 1995, p. 4).

Part of the reason this discussion appears in Chapter 8 is because the Jamal group made a big mistake. They did not consider how they might draw others into their work or how they might export their ideas to others until the outside world thrust itself upon their team. There is no need for middle school teams to make the same mistake. Dealing with boundaries is especially important when people are members of multiple groups (Ancona & Caldwell, 1988), as is clearly the case among middle school teachers, who find themselves working on teams, participating as members of academic departments, serving on school committees, and so on.

One study of team behavior (Kain, 1997a) involved interviews with many middle school team members, asking them to describe a time when their team worked together successfully to create an integrated learning experience for their students. Their answers are insightful, worth exploring in another context. But the follow-up question, asking them how they related to the rest of the school and how the school responded to their work, revealed a fascinating and frightening aspect of teamwork in middle schools. All too often the answer to this question sounded something like one teacher's response: "We felt ostracized by the other teams. We were called the crazy team. When we were successful, it didn't settle well with other teachers. Because other teachers... my perception at this school was 'it's okay if you do something different, but at the point that I perceive that I look bad and you look good then I don't like it anymore.'" Another teacher said, "The minute it started getting good – this always, always plagued me! – the minute we really started getting excellence, we started experiencing professional jealousy." These kinds of answers reveal the significant problems teams face even in (perhaps especially in) their successes. The comments also portray a tendency for teamed teachers to assume victim roles, as though injustices were "done" to them and they had no part in the events. That's the mistake that is eminently preventable. Thus, this chapter.

Consider the Jamal group's work as an example. They did work through a lot of personal issues; they did come to a consensus regarding their purpose; they did develop fairly effective norms and procedures and they did manage to resolve their conflict positively. All the signs of a good team, right? But then the drawing of their "horse" somehow slipped into the public domain. The big secret this "elite" group (groups perceived as holding some secret are generally labeled "elite") had been working on surfaced, and a lot of resentful people had the opportunity to guffaw at the expense of some very naive but sincere team members. Fundamentally, there were two surprises here that didn't belong. First, the Jamal team members shouldn't have been surprised at the responses of their compatriots because they should have been in touch with the public sentiments much sooner. Second, the public shouldn't have been surprised at the work of the Jamal group because the team should have been laying the foundations for the acceptance and support of its work from the very start. As McIntosh-Fletcher (1996) observed in studying business teams, "Shared teaming involves not only integrating team members' work, but also linking the work of the team with other teams and other parts of the organization" (p. 34).

A metaphoric framework for boundary issues

Some of the most useful insight into boundary issues as they relate to middle school teams has come from the work of Deborah Ancona and David Caldwell (Ancona, 1990; Ancona & Caldwell, 1988), even though it does not address middle school teams directly. These researchers have examined how teams relate to other groups and important persons in the context of new product development teams and department of education consulting teams. From this work, they have developed a metaphoric map for effective boundary relations that can provide a framework to assist teams.

Ancona and Caldwell (1988) describe four perspectives for boundary spanning, each with an accompanying set of activities: *scout, ambassador, guard,* and *sentry* (Figure 6). These roles or perspectives will form the basis of a planning activity for teams.

Figure 6: Boundary-spanning Activities
(based on Ancona & Caldwell, 1988).

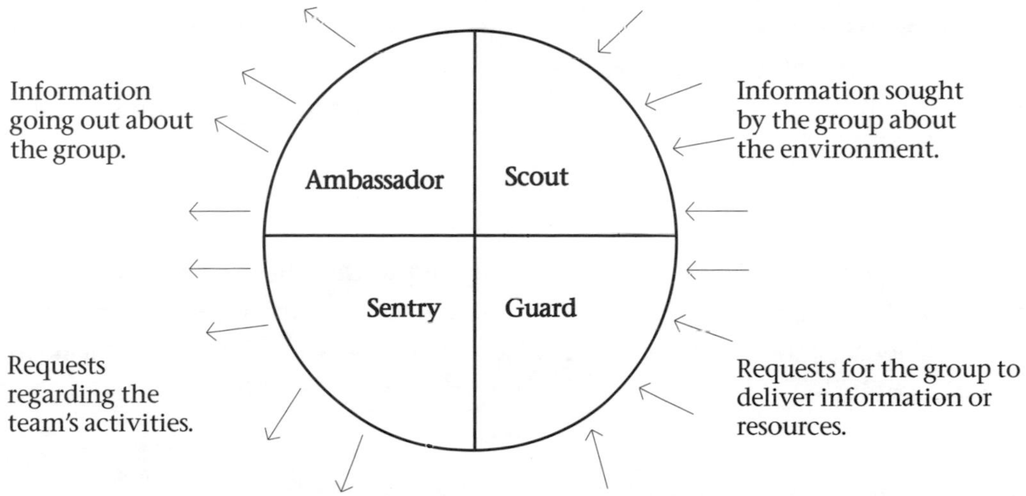

Information going out about the group.

Information sought by the group about the environment.

Ambassador — Scout

Sentry — Guard

Requests regarding the team's activities.

Requests for the group to deliver information or resources.

The circle in the diagram represents the team itself. The four quadrants represent roles that team members assume in effectively relating to outsiders.

Scout activities, according to Ancona and Caldwell (1988), are those which encourage team members to attend to the environment in which the team works, to bring in information (hence the arrows in the diagram). How are others perceiving the work of this team? Who are our allies and opponents? What key players do we need to get on our side? What changes occurring in the school or system will influence our work? These and other questions demonstrate that teams can actively seek information (to be able to do something about it) rather than being knocked over by the consequences of not having the information.

Here's an example from a middle school team. In the spring of a school year, an eighth-grade team was meeting to plan its work for the following year. On his way to the meeting, the science teacher on this team encountered the principal, who asked what the meeting was all about. When the science teacher explained, the principal casually remarked, "Sounds good, *if* you are together next year." The science teacher, true to the "scout" role, took that information back to his team, which began an active lobbying campaign for its survival based on this information.

As a "scout," a team member might engage in a constant scanning of the environment, focusing on such issues as a "map" of the social terrain (who stands where on the work we're doing?). A scout might also be attuned to changes in the school or district that would influence the success or survival of the team. For example, the work being done "downtown" on a new social studies curriculum could have powerful consequences for the team's attempts to integrate curricula. Good scouts even notice things that don't seem directly related to the work of the team, but represent potential trouble spots. Scouts seek feedback from others about how the team's work is being perceived. The essence of scouting is bringing to the group information and resources to assist the team in accomplishing its purpose. Hargreaves (1995) calls this "understanding the political configuration of your school" (p. 18). And schools like everything else these days, have a political side. The scout should be sensitive to school-related "letters to the editor," reports on the results of state-wide testing, the speeches about education made by various national and state leaders, the development of subject standards, and other such education-related activities.

Ambassador activities are those actions team members take to *export* information from the group. Ancona and Caldwell (1988) highlight four different forms of this:

- the initial opening of channels of communication,
- informing others of the team's progress,
- coordinating the team's work with others (for example, negotiating the schedule for using buses for a field trip), and
- "molding" the environment – actively attempting to alter beliefs or practices of others.

A good example of this kind of activity occurred on the same middle school team described above. When the team members realized not only that their team composition was in question, but also that the practice of teaming at this particular school was threatened, they became "ambassadors for teaming." They arranged a meeting with the seventh-grade teachers in order to extol the virtues of teaming, to explain all the wonderful things teaming had done for them and their students. The ostensible goal for their presentation was to get their colleagues to try team teaching arrangements; but at a more personal level, they knew that if they couldn't change the behavior of these teachers, they might at least alter the teachers' beliefs enough to get support for teaming at the school. As the social studies teacher put it, "we have to sell teaming." The rumor among the teachers at this school was that "teaming drives the timetable," a mistaken perception, but one that provided a lot of ammunition for the anti-team folks. After all, if your teaming means I have a less desirable preparation period, I'm not likely to support you – UNLESS you've done a great job as ambassador for the team.

My own bias is that this is the most important boundary issue requiring attention. Too often teams think they're doing something effective by "hiding" their ideas and work until the big, splashy presentation occurs. Instead, people in the school begin to wonder what's going on, to suspect the worst, to foster jealousies and resentment, even to wish for the failure of the team. The work of middle school teams is far too important to risk this! The best chance of success for the team is to begin boundary spanning when it begins to meet. Open channels of communication: contact key players (parent leaders, other teams, administrators) just to let them know who you are and how you can stay in touch. Inform others of what you're doing even before you have any "big" projects to boast about: send home newsletters, put memos in the principal's box, inform the central office of your work.

Consider how you can negotiate for materials and resources you want without antagonizing your colleagues. Team members in one middle school found themselves angry and envious when another team came up with the excellent idea of placing team bulletin boards in the hallway of the seventh-grade wing. The problem was that one team used up all the wall space, leaving nothing for the other two teams. Sure, the idea "belonged" to a particular team, but the consequences in this case were resentment and an atmosphere of secretive competition between teamed teachers, hardly the sort of thing that makes a whole school successful. Here's a case where the ambassador role of coordinating and negotiating could have brought success all around instead of undermining the larger purpose of teaming – creating a great school. Finally, work to mold the environment in which you work. Passively accepting anything that comes your way is not the route to team success. Instead, use your combined empowerment to do what's best for your kids. Wasley (1995) relates how a team of high school teachers was able to win the support of the rest of their faculty by regularly sharing successes and trials.

The last two roles outlined by Ancona and Caldwell (1988) also offer team members help in establishing successful relations with those outside the team. The role of **team sentry** focuses on responding to information and resources outsiders want to send into your team. For example, when someone tells the team members they need to read a particular book, the sentry role involves legitimately taking charge to decide if this is something the team needs. Someone else says that your team ought to administer a learning-styles inventory because that's the only way to find out what we need to know to meet student needs. Another person wants the team to focus everything on "multiple intelligences." I knew a middle school team that had to sit through one parent's endless presentation on how teachers ought to present information to young people in lectures (one team member noted that this parent would have been run out of a middle school class in the first five minutes!). There is always someone who wants to impose something on a team. The sentry role allows teams to decide whether or not this imposition deserves entry into the team. A more refined role for sentries is to translate the ideas of outsiders into terms that are meaningful and relevant or to filter larger bits of information so that the team receives a manageable amount. For example, when a science department appears to resist a team's request for materials, it may be that the science teacher on the team can present that information in terms that help the team members to appreciate the reasons for resistance.

The **guard role** takes the complementary position to that of the sentry. There will be occasions when people and groups will make requests of a team for information, resources, or services. Teams need to realize that they exercise a legitimate control over such requests. The "guard" perspective involves classifying requests so that the team can either deliver the request when appropriate or protect the team (Ancona & Caldwell, 1988). For example, I worked with one middle school team on a variety of teaming issues to help them improve their effectiveness. In the middle of our work together, the team informed me that their principal expected them to do a presentation about teaming for the whole faculty. How often we see this! "You've had some training on how to team, so you can just take an hour or so to teach the rest of us." Obviously this happens to individuals as well as teams. But the key consideration here is whether or not the request is appropriate for the team, and what the consequences of delivering might be. I suspect that this "do-a-presentation-for-us" mentality trivializes the real struggles we all make to learn something new. And I know that making a team do a presentation prematurely can threaten that team's effectiveness (on various levels). The guard role says to this principal's request, "That's an issue we need to discuss as a team. We'll let you know what we think we should do." The guard then raises the issue with the team, and the team together decides how to respond.

In conceiving of boundary issues in terms of *scout, ambassador, sentry,* and *guard* teams can be empowered to move beyond victim status. Teams can realize it is legitimate, even necessary, to say *no* to some requests. Teams can actively seek ways to enhance their relations with outsiders.

Activities

After developing an awareness of the importance of boundary considerations, the next important step is for a real team to personalize the matter. To assist in this, I've provided a set of questions to help teams examine their own boundary relations. These questions are divided into two groups. I recommend teams deal with both sets of questions, ideally in two different sessions.

Set one: a look at team boundary spanning.

1. What boundary issues has the team faced in the past year? (For example, have there been requests made of the team? Has the team had opportunities to provide others with information? What reputation is the team developing?)

2. What boundary issues do you anticipate in the next year? (For example, what important persons and groups will the team need to develop relations with? What persons and groups will attempt to influence the team or should the team attempt to influence? What changes in the school environment could affect the team?)

3. What are three goals the team can set in relation to boundary issues that will help the team achieve its overall purpose?

4. What are some of the other important groups (for example, subject departments) that team members are a part of? How can the team be sensitive to competing demands?

Set two: the scout, ambassador, sentry and guard roles.

1. In terms of the above roles, what do you see as your strongest area?

2. In terms of those roles, what do you see as each of your team members' strengths?

3. As a scout, what would you identify as noteworthy key spots in your social terrain?

4. From the perspective of an ambassador, what do you see as the most important "exports" your team has to offer?

5. Thinking as a sentry, what kinds of information or expectations do you see others imposing on your team? How should the team respond to them?

6. As a guard, what requests do you see being made of your team to provide information or service? What are some productive ways of saying *no*?

Final word

Boundary spanners sometimes experience more stress than others (Ancona & Caldwell, 1988), so team members ought to be sensitive to this and stay in close communication. In fact, it would be a healthy practice for teams, regardless of who may take on the roles of scout, ambassador, sentry and guard, to discuss regularly how the team is relating to outsiders. You want to avoid becoming successful "islands in the stream" (Mills, Powell, & Pollak, 1992). Here's a place where good leadership can be asserted. It is in its ignoring of boundaries that the Jamal group finds its work and its very existence threatened. Instead, work for your team's success through effective boundary management. Of course, it would be naive to assume that the team can completely control relationships with all the forces in a school. As team members, you should take charge and do what you can to relate well to others. However, the power of the organization is not easily ignored. Donnellon (1996) writes about the "heroic" struggle teams make in most organizations due to the new work roles inherent in teaming. Organizations which require team work "must accommodate themselves to the requirements of team work. To assimilate teams into the existing categories of the bureaucratic organization . . . is to gain little from a change that, even if minimally implemented, disturbs the status quo" (Donnellon, 1996, p. 234). Interviews with middle school teachers demonstrate that conditions within the organization (school) do much to promote or impede teams' success (Kain, 1997a). A middle school considering teacher teaming must carefully address how the organization will promote or prevent effective teaming.

9.

"It's Not a Horse. It's a Camel!"

Celebrating Team Accomplishments

The minutes

Dina: It seems we've got the horse done. It's ready to survive the desert. It's ready to help our people.

Rachel: It can be a source of milk or meat.

Berodak: It can travel long distances without much water.

Sichem: It's a little bit ugly.

Dina: It is functional.

Rachel: Don't forget it can also carry heavy loads.

Berodak: And we've got several variations now.

Melchuzar: I think we might consider ourselves finished.

Sichem: Are you serious? We're done?

Berodak: Seems pretty complete to me.

Sichem: But I'm not sure I want to be done. I bet there's more we can do.

Melchuzar: As certain as there will be sand in tents. There will always be more to do, but there is not always time to do more. For whatever flaws still remain, the time has come to call our work complete.

Rachel: So we can go. I guess this is it.

Dina: Just like that? It doesn't seem right.

Melchuzar: Indeed it is not right.

Sichem: So, back to work. How about a flap for shade? It sort of rises from the tail. That's it. It's part of the tail, only it broadens out like, like . . . like this bird I once saw.

Melchuzar: Slow down, Sichem. You misunderstand me. I do think it is time to finish our work.

Sichem: But you said—

Melchuzar: I said it was not right. Not right just to end, to walk away, to forget about what we've done. We have accomplished a marvelous thing here. We have designed the beast of perfection.

Berodak: What a horse!

Dina: But, it's not really a horse is it? I mean it's different enough that it almost feels funny calling it a horse.

Rachel: That's right. It needs some other name.

Berodak: Is that a part of our job? I mean, weren't we supposed to design this perfect horse?

Melchuzar: Indeed, we have.

Berodak: So, we don't really have the liberty to change what we call it. We could make it a special kind of horse.

Dina: But it's not a horse. It's simply too different to call it by the same name.

Sichem: Horskin. Horsloom. Horstick. Horscam.

Dina: Or leave off the horse altogether. What about a completely new name?

Sichem: Horslet. Horssel.

Dina: Are you listening? It's not a horse! It's a—

Berodak: Camel!

Dina: What?

A consideration for every team at some point is how to end their work together. In the Jamal group, there is a natural ending point. The job is done. For school teams, each year provides an opportunity to reconsider team membership. Remember first, that teams take time to develop. Don't be too hasty to end your team work. Second, if you do break apart, give attention to how you do this. Allow yourselves an event to mark the breakup.

Berodak: Camel. Why not. I just took a couple of Sichem's syllables and it seems like the right word.

Sichem: Camel?

Dina: Camel.

Melchuzar: Perfect. My last discomfort is settled. We truly can call our work done. And since the work is done, it is time to celebrate the work.

Sichem: A party?

Melchuzar: Of course. A party such as you've never seen before.

Sichem: Is that all right for us to do?

Dina: Can we?

Melchuzar: How can we not? We would be committing a great wrong to walk away without this. In fact, I've already arranged it. Come along.

Commentary

We haven't seen all the notes from the Jamal group, but we've seen enough to catch some inspiration. Teams are not just an administrative convenience. Teams are to turn us into camel-makers!

The final section of the Jamal notes demonstrates one final and very important concept about effective teaming: celebrating teams and the work they do. One of the traditions we need to overturn in schools is the isolated, fragmented teacher. Staff social activities and committee work do something to ease this isolation, but only in the most superficial way. For the rest, it seems that we still look to the individual "hero" when we think of teacher evaluation or recognition and rewards. Model teachers from the movies – in sync with the view of the wider public – "gain their reputations in contradiction to, rather than in collaboration with, the schools in which they teach" (Cook, 1995, p. 40). We simply don't acknowledge the team player at this level.

In this final examination of the Jamal script, I'd like to draw parallels to two issues of importance to teams. Evaluation and rewards, though not directly addressed in the Jamal notes as we see them, are an important factor in work. What can we do to enhance teams' effectiveness in relation to these important issues? And the second issue is celebration. Beyond the formal system of evaluation and recognition, how can teams build for themselves the practice of celebrating their accomplishments? The Jamal script appropriately ends with the beginning of a party!

Rewards and evaluations

While there appears to be some movement in business toward appraising workers as team members (Parker, 1994; Wellins et al., 1991), there is no comparable movement in education. It's an unfortunate reality that even in the schools that are most supportive of teaming, teacher evaluation still tends to be an exercise in independence. Of course, evaluation is fraught with misunderstandings anyway. One math teacher was helping her students learn to use a software program when her supervisor came to evaluate her. He announced to her that he would "come back later, when you are teaching something." It is no wonder, in a system that fosters that sort of remark, that the team behavior of teachers remains unexamined and probably unappreciated by evaluators.

Teamwork is *work*, and a typical individual response to unacknowledged teamwork is this: "Why should I knock myself out doing work for this team when none of what I do here gets included in my annual performance appraisal?" (Parker, 1994, p. 103). As long as team behavior is treated like an add-on to the real work of teaching, it will remain marginally important. How, then, can we help to solve this problem?

Two considerations might help in the move toward more reasonable and more team-based evaluations. First, recall the ambassador function of team members in managing their boundaries (Chapter 8). Teams can literally mold the environment in which they find themselves. This is especially true of multiple teams. One way to influence the way teachers are evaluated is for teams to begin lobbying their administrators and professional associations to acknowledge the importance of teamwork in teacher evaluations. Suggest the kinds of behaviors you find valuable to your teams (like following through on commitments, attending and contributing to meetings, sharing in the duties of the team, learning new techniques and concepts to make connections, working for our purpose, and so on) as indicators of effective teaming with which evaluators can credit teachers. Encourage your evaluators to learn more about teaming, to read about the practice, to incorporate teaming concepts into their understanding of effective teaching.

Second, do not underestimate the importance of evaluations within the team. That is, team members can provide very meaningful evaluations of each other. Harvey & Drolet (1994) speak of bombarding team members with strengths – a session devoted to verbalizing the good things you see in each other. While this sort of evaluation is institutionally weak, it is the kind of powerful motivator that makes work personally meaningful (Hackman & Oldham, 1980). Likewise, honestly letting your colleagues know when they are not producing or when they should reconsider their membership on the team can make the experience more personally meaningful. In fact, your team should work to hold members accountable to one another for the team's performance. Recall the Katzenbach and Smith (1993, p. 45) definition: "A team is a small number of people with complementary skills who are committed to a common purpose, performance goals, and approach for which they hold themselves mutually accountable." The "Charge for Team" (Figure 2, p. 14) includes a place for your team to describe an agreed-upon plan for holding all team members accountable.

If teams in the business world are moving toward team appraisal, they are still a long way from team pay; although a few teamed organizations are experimenting with ways of compensating workers for their teamwork. Practices like "gainsharing" and pay-for-skill (Parker, 1994) are examples of this. Is such an approach necessary for teachers? Clearly, if we were to ask teachers if they would like more money for their work on teams, odds are they would say *yes*. However, it may not be a crucial factor. Let me explain.

It is fairly well documented that teachers find the reward of teaching to be largely in the sense of accomplishment associated with successful learning experiences for their students (Lortie, 1975). In other words, it is not just a question of money. Of course, that's true in the world of business as well. Workers do appreciate intangible rewards, such as recognition (Parker, 1994), motivational events (Wellins et al., 1991) and the satisfaction of a good "fit" between their job demands and interests (Hackman & Oldham, 1980; Culbert & McDonough, 1980). In fact, Kohn (1993) argues that any special reward for performance is destined to be ineffective and that "The surest way to destroy teamwork, and therefore organizational excellence, is to make rewards scarce – that is, make people compete" (p. 137).

The reward associated with teaming may be a motivating, but intangible reward. It's not uncommon for teamed teachers to make statements like the following comments from a middle school science teacher and a middle school English teacher: "It's one of the best things about being at this school for me. I'd only consider other jobs if I could take my team with me." "If they take away teaming, I'm out of here." Clearly, teaming provides its own reward. Teacher collaboration can reduce teacher isolation (Mills, Powell, & Pollak, 1992) and bring career rewards (Inger, 1993), making the working world for teachers more enjoyable. Teaming can improve the professional self-image of teachers (Gatewood, Cline, Green, & Harris, 1992). In other words, there is a reward for teaming, even if it can't be deposited in a bank.

Team identity through celebrating

A more positive issue for finishing our look at the Jamal script focuses on the less business-like topic of celebration. I've already stated that teams can do some valuable work through their evaluation of members. In the same way, teams can enhance their success through their own embrace of celebrating their work together. Harvey and Drolet (1994) put it this way:

> *Joyful environments are more productive than joyless ones. When individuals understand each other as people and have the opportunity to enter into relationships, they feel more like colleagues and team members. All those potlucks and staff parties and retreats and recognition lunches and TGIF gatherings are important. As with affability, they are not sufficient. But they are necessary.* (p. 20)

Middle school theorists have pointed out the importance of such things as team names, team symbols, and slogans (Erb & Doda, 1989; Merenbloom, 1991). But their focus has been on the importance of such devices for the students. Without diminishing that in the least, I would like to emphasize that these same devices can be of great importance to teachers on teams. Stories of outstandingly successful teams in the business world often include the use of slogans, symbols, and other identity markers. For example, Rayner (1993) tells of the importance of symbols to the team developing new instrument controllers at Z-technology. The "pepper project" used posters, mugs, T-shirts, and nicknames from the movie *Top Gun* to inspire and reward team members. Katzenbach & Smith (1993, p. 141) document the way "constructive reinforcement fuels the mutual accountability and confidence so critical to team performance" with examples such as the "Zebra" team at Kodak, which "created Zebra costumes, cheers, slogans, and songs to constantly reinforce their commitment to black and white products." Many more examples from the business world make it clear that the use of symbols is not a juvenile practice, not something only for middle school *kids,* but a solid way of bringing unity, common vision, and fun to the work of adults.

In fact, the notion of fun may be the best place to end this exploration into camel-making. Teams ought to be fun; teaching ought to be more successful and more enjoyable because of the use of teams. And teams should not wait for someone else to make them have fun – having fun ought to be a priority for teams from the start. This can be in the context of work, but it can be especially effective as it extends beyond the work situation. For example, the "Dallas Mafia," a team of investment bankers, made wine together to enjoy one another (Katzenbach & Smith, 1993). Making connections outside of work can help teamed teachers become more cohesive and more effective. Of course, this must be tempered with the other demands placed on the lives of team members. It would be unjust and ineffective to ask a team to replace the social life of its members.

Within the world of work, it is crucial that teams achieve and celebrate victories, small and large. Parker (1994) tells teams "that if they wait for the organization to provide recognition, they may be very disappointed" (p. 132). Therefore, what are some ways you can begin to celebrate? Try some of these ideas:

- Devise rewards for each team member. Consider the strengths each person brings to your joint work, and build the rewards around those. For example, one team member I know is fabulous at bringing her team back to the agenda in a positive manner when they start to wander off. Everyone appreciates her tact and skill. She deserves the *Agenda Herder and Nurturer Award!*

- Publicize your accomplishments. Parents and administrators want to know what's happening in your team. But if you wait for someone to come interview you and do a write-up, you may never be "discovered." Instead, take initiative in telling others the good things you are doing. If you can't get an entry into someone's newsletter, it's time to produce your own!

- Organize parties to mark your achievements. This doesn't have to be the sort of party you have when the team is identified as "team of the year for the entire state." You've made it through the first three weeks of school and your students see you as a team. That's worth celebrating! You just completed the first attempt at integrating your curricula around a three-day problem activity. That's worth celebrating! You've negotiated common rules for all your students. That's at least worth cookies at lunch. The point is to find ways to acknowledge, at least within your own team, the good things you are doing.

List three opportunities you have recently missed, things you should have celebrated in your team, but did not do so. (If you're just starting, think about some of your past life as a team member.) Discuss what was worthy of celebrating in these events. Use this as inspiration for the future. You can find the successes to fuel celebration.

The working world of teachers has undervalued collaboration. I hope that this examination of the work of the world's most famous committee can inspire your team to become camel-makers. Remember, you can do something new, something great together. **Take charge!**

Jamal Anticipators

A Bibliography

Adams, J. L. (1979). *Conceptual blockbusting: A guide to better ideas.* (2nd ed.). New York: W.W. Norton & Company.

Ahlgren, A., & Kesidou, S. (1995). Attempting curriculum coherence in Project 2061. In J.A. Beane, (Ed.), *Toward a coherent curriculum,* (pp. 44-54). Alexandria, VA: Association for Supervision and Curriculum Development.

Ancona, D. G. (1990). Outward bound: Strategies for team survival in an organization. *Academy of Management Journal, 23* (2), 334-365.

Ancona, D. G. & Caldwell, D. F. (1988). Beyond task and maintenance: Defining external functions in groups. *Group & Organizational Studies, 13* (4), 468-494.

Bakhtin, M. M. (1981). *The dialogic imagination: Four essays.* (C. Emerson & M. Holquist, Trans.). (M. Holquist, Ed.). Austin, TX: University of Texas.

Beane, J. A. (1993). *A middle school curriculum: From rhetoric to reality.* (2nd ed.). Columbus, OH: National Middle School Association.

Beane, J. A. (1995a). Curriculum integration and the disciplines of knowledge. *Phi Delta Kappan, 76* (8), 617-622.

Beane, J. A. (Ed.). (1995b). *Toward a coherent curriculum.* Alexandria, VA: Association for Supervision and Curriculum Development.

Beane, J.A. (1997). *Curriculum integration: Designing the core of democratic education.* New York: Teachers College Press.

Cook, A. (1995, March 8). Teachers as team players: Or, how many heroes does it take to change a school? *Education Week,* 40, 30.

Culbert, S. A., & McDonough, J. J. (1980). *The invisible war: Pursuing self-interests at work.* New York: Wiley.

Cummings, T. G. (1981). Designing effective work groups. In P. C. Nydstrom & W. H. Starbuck, (Eds.), *Handbook of organizational design. Volume 2: Remodeling organizations and their environments* (pp. 252-271). New York: Oxford University Press.

Dickinson, T. S., & Erb, T. O. (Eds.). (1997). *We gain more than we give: Teaming in middle schools*. Columbus, OH: National Middle School Association.

Donnellon, A. (1996). *Team talk: The power of language in team dynamics*. Boston: Harvard Business School.

Douglass, M. E., & Douglass, D. N. (1992). *Time management for teams*. New York: AMACOM.

Doyle, W., & Ponder, G. A. (1977-78). The practicality ethic in teacher decision-making. *Interchange, 8* (3) 1-12.

Dyer, W. G. (1995). *Team building: Current issues and new alternatives* (3rd ed.). (Part of Addison-Wesley Series on Organization Development, Eds., Edgar H. Schein and Richard Beckhard). Reading, MA: Addison-Wesley.

Erb, T. O. (1997). Thirty years of attempting to fathom teaming: Battling pot-holes and hairpin curves along the way. In T. S. Dickinson & T. O. Erb (Eds.), *We gain more than we give: Teaming in middle schools*, (pp. 19-59). Columbus, OH: National Middle School Association.

Erb, T. O., & Doda, N. M. (1989). *Team organization: Promise—practices and possibilities*. Washington, D.C.: National Education Association.

Fisher, K. (1993). *Leading self-directed work teams: A guide to developing new team leadership skills*. New York: McGraw-Hill.

Gatewood, T. E., Cline, G., Green, G., & Harris, S. E. (1992). Middle school interdisciplinary team organization and its relationship to teacher stress. *Research in Middle Level Education, 15* (2), 27-40.

George, P. S. (1982). Interdisciplinary team organization: Four operational phases. *Middle School Journal, 13* (3), 10-13.

Gersick, C. J. G. (1989). Marking time: Predictable transitions in task groups. *Academy of Management Journal, 32* (2), 274-309.

Glasgow, N. A. (1997). *New curriculum for new times: A guide to student-centered, problem-based learning*. Thousand Oaks, CA: Corwin.

Grant, L. (1994, February 18). New jewel in the crown. *U.S. News & World Report*, 55-57.

Hackman, J. R. (Ed.). (1990). *Groups that work (and those that don't): Creating conditions for effective teamwork*. San Francisco: Jossey-Bass.

Hackman, J. R., & Morris, C. G. (1975). Group tasks, group interaction process, and group performance effectiveness: A review and proposed integration. In L. Berkowitz, (Ed.), *Advances in Experimental Social Psychology, Vol. 8* (pp. 45-90). New York: Academic.

Hackman, J. R., & Oldham, G. R. (1980). *Work redesign.* Reading, MA: Addison-Wesley.

Hackman, J. R., & Walton, R. E. (1986). Leading groups in organizations. In P. S. Goodman (Ed.), *Designing effective work groups,* (pp. 72-119). San Francisco: Jossey-Bass.

Hargreaves, A. (1995). Renewal in the age of paradox. *Educational Leadership, 52* (7), 14-19.

Harvey, T. R., & Drolet, B. (1994). *Building teams, building people: Expanding the fifth resource.* Lancaster, PA: Technomic.

Hirschhorn, L. (1991). *Managing in the new team environment: Skills, tools, and methods.* (Part of Addison-Wesley Series on Organization Development, Eds., Edgar H. Schein and Richard Beckhard). Reading, MA: Addison-Wesley.

Hoffman, L.R. (1982). Improving the problem-solving process in managerial groups. In R.A. Guzzo (Ed.), *Improving group decision making in organizations: Approaches from theory and research.* New York: Academic Press.

Inger, M. (1993). *Teacher collaboration in secondary schools. Centerfocus Number 2.* National Center for Research in Vocational Education. (ERIC Reproduction Services Document No. ED364733)

Irvin, J. L. (Ed.). (1997). *What current research says to the middle level practitioner.* Columbus, OH: National Middle School Association.

Jacobs, H. H. (1997). *Mapping the big picture: Integrating curriculum & assessment K-12.* Alexandria, VA: Association for Supervision and Curriculum Development.

Johnson, D. W., & Johnson, F. P. (1994). *Joining together: Group theory and group skills* (5th ed.). Boston: Allyn and Bacon.

Johnston, S. (1995). Curriculum decision making at the school level: Is it just a case of teachers learning to act like administrators? *Journal of Curriculum and Supervision, 10* (2), 136-154.

Joyce, B., & Weil, M. (with B. Showers). (1992). *Models of teaching* (4th ed.). Englewood Cliffs, N.J.: Prentice-Hall.

Kain, D. L. (1992). *Collaborative planning of interdisciplinary experiences: A case study at the middle school level.* Unpublished doctoral dissertation, The University of British Columbia, Vancouver.

Kain, D. L. (1993). Deciding to integrate curricula: Judgments about holding and stretching. *Research in Middle Level Education, 16* (2), 25-41.

Kain, D. L. (1997a). Critical incidents in teacher collaboration on interdisciplinary teams. *Research in Middle Level Education Quarterly, 21* (1), 1-29.

Kain, D. L. (1997b). Misplaced camels, crowded captains, and achieving greatness: Leadership of interdisciplinary teams. In T. S. Dickinson & T. O. Erb (Eds.), *We gain more than we give: Teaming in middle schools,* (pp. 403-424). Columbus, OH: National Middle School Association.

Katzenbach, J. R., & Smith, D. K. (1993). *The wisdom of teams: Creating the high-performance organization.* Boston: Harvard Business School.

Kohn, A. (1993). *Punished by rewards: The trouble with gold stars, incentive plans, A's, praise, and other bribes.* Boston: Houghton Mifflin.

Kruse, S., & Louis, K. S. (1995). Teacher teaming—Opportunities and dilemmas. *Brief to principals* (11). Madison, WI: Center on Organization and Restructuring of Schools.

Lortie, D. C. (1975). *Schoolteacher: A sociological study.* Chicago: University of Chicago.

Maeroff, G. I. (1993). Building teams to rebuild schools. *Phi Delta Kappan, 74* (7), 512-519.

McGrath, J.E. (1984). *Groups: Interaction and performance.* Englewood Cliffs, NJ: Prentice Hall.

McIntosh-Fletcher, D. (1996). *Teaming by design: Real teams for real people.* Chicago: Irwin.

Merenbloom, E. Y. (1991). *The team process: A handbook for teachers.* (3rd ed.) Columbus, OH: National Middle School Association.

Mills, R. A., Powell, R. R., & Pollak, J. P. (1992). The influence of middle level interdisciplinary teaming on teacher isolation: A case study. *Research in Middle Level Education, 15* (2), 9-25.

Mitchell, R. (1986). Team building by disclosure of internal frames of reference. *Journal of Applied Behavioral Science, 22* (1), 15-28.

Oakes, J., Vasudeva, A., & Jones, M. (1996). Becoming educative: Reforming curriculum and teaching in the middle grades. *Research in Middle Level Education Quarterly, 20* (1), 11-40.

Parker, G. M. (1994). *Cross-functional teams: Working with allies, enemies and other strangers.* San Francisco: Jossey-Bass.

Porod, G. N. (1993). New roles for teachers: Instructional team leaders. *Schools in the Middle, 3*(2), 7-10.

Rayner, S. R. (1993). *Recreating the workplace: The pathway to high performance work systems.* Essex Junction, NJ: Oliver Wight.

Savoie, J.M., & Hughes, A.S. (1994). Problem-based learning as classroom solution. *Educational Leadership, 52*(3), 54-57.

Senge, P. M. (1990). *The fifth discipline: The art and practice of the learning organization.* New York: Doubleday.

Springer, M. (1994). *Watershed: A successful voyage into integrative learning.* Columbus, OH: National Middle School Association.

Steiner, I. D. (1970). *Group process and productivity.* New York: Academic.

Stepien, W., & Gallagher, S. (1993). Problem-based learning: As authentic as it gets. *Educational Leadership, 50*(7), 25-28.

Strahan, D., Bowles, N., Richardson, V., & Hanawald, S. (1997). Research on teaming: Insights from selected studies. In T. S. Dickinson & T. O. Erb (Eds.), *We gain more than we give: Teaming in middle schools,* (pp. 359-384). Columbus, OH: National Middle School Association.

Tuckman, B. W. (1965). Developmental sequence in small groups. *Psychological Bulletin, 63*(6), 384-399.

Wasley, P. A. (1995). Straight shooting. *Educational Leadership, 52*(7), 56-58.

Wellins, R. S., Byham, W. C., & Wilson, J. M. (1991). *Empowered teams: Creating self-directed work groups that improve quality, productivity, and participation.* San Francisco: Jossey-Bass.

Wellins, R. S., Byham, W. C., & Dixon, G. R. (1994). *Inside teams: How 20 world-class organizations are winning through teamwork.* San Francisco: Jossey-Bass

Wheatley, M. J. (1992). *Leadership and the new science: Learning about organization from an orderly universe.* San Francisco: Berret-Koehler.

Whitford, B. L., & Kyle, D. W. (April, 1984). *Interdisciplinary teaming: Initiating change in a middle school.* Paper presented at the annual meeting of the American Educational Research Association. New Orleans. (ERIC Document Reproduction Service No. ED 263 672)

Wiggins, G. (1995). Curricular coherence and assessment: Making sure that the effect matches the intent. In J. A. Beane, (Ed.), *Toward a coherent curriculum,* (pp. 101-119). Alexandria, VA: Association for Supervision and Curriculum Development.

Worchel, S., Coutant-Sassic, D., & Wong, F. (1993). Toward a more balanced view of conflict: There is a positive side. In S. Worchel & J. A. Simpson (Eds.), *Conflict between people & groups: Causes, processes, and resolutions* (pp. 76-89). Chicago: Nelson-Hall.

National Middle School Association

National Middle School Association, established in 1973, is the voice for professionals and others interested in the education and well-being of young adolescents. The association has grown rapidly and enrolls members in all 50 states, the Canadian provinces, and 42 other nations. In addition, 57 state, regional, and provincial middle school associations are official affiliates of NMSA.

NMSA is the only national association dedicated exclusively to the education, development, and growth of young adolescents. Membership is open to all. While middle level teachers and administrators make up the bulk of the membership, central office personnel, college and university faculty, state department officials, other professionals, parents, and lay citizens are members and active in supporting our single mission — improving the educational experiences of 10-15 year olds. This open and diverse membership is a particular strength of NMSA's.

The association publishes *Middle School Journal*, the movement's premier professional journal; *Research in Middle Level Education Online*; *Middle Ground, the Magazine of Middle Level Education*; *Target*, the association's newsletter; *The Family Connection*, a newsletter for families; *Classroom Connections*, a practical quarterly resource; and a series of research summaries.

A leading publisher of professional books and monographs in the field of middle level education, NMSA provides resources both for understanding and advancing various aspects of the middle school concept and for assisting classroom teachers in planning for instruction. More than 70 NMSA publications are available through the resource catalog as well as selected titles published by other organizations.

The association's highly acclaimed Annual Conference, which has drawn approximately 10,000 registrants in recent years, is each year in the fall. NMSA also sponsors many other professional development opportunities.

For information about NMSA and its many services, contact the association's headquarters office at 4151 Executive Parkway, Suite 300, Westerville, Ohio, 43081. TELEPHONE: 800-528-NMSA; FAX: 618-895-4750; INTERNET: www.nmsa.org.